From a Slab of Clay

From a Slab of Clay

Daryl E. Baird

Published by
The American Ceramic Society
600 Cleveland Avenue, Suite 210
Westerville, Ohio 43082 USA

The American Ceramic Society
600 N. Cleveland Ave., Suite 210
Westerville, OH 43082

© 2012 by The American Ceramic Society, All rights reserved.

ISBN: 978-1-57498-317-3 (Paperback)

ISBN: 978-1-57498-502-3 (PDF)

Second printing 2013

No part of this book may be reproduced, stored in a retrieval system or transmitted in any form or by any means, electronic, mechanical, photocopying, microfilming, recording or otherwise, without written permission from the publisher, except by a reviewer, who may quote brief passages in review.

Authorization to photocopy for internal or personal use beyond the limits of Sections 107 and 108 of the U.S. Copyright Law is granted by The American Ceramic Society, provided that the appropriate fee is paid directly to the Copyright Clearance Center, Inc., 222 Rosewood Drive, Danvers, MA 01923 U.S.A., www.copyright.com. Prior to photocopying items for educational classroom use, please contact Copyright Clearance Center, Inc. This consent does not extend to copyright items for general distribution or for advertising or promotional purposes or to republishing items in whole or in part in any work in any format. Requests for special photocopying permission and reprint requests should be directed to Director, Publications, The American Ceramic Society, 600 N. Cleveland Ave., Westerville, Ohio 43082 USA.

Every effort has been made to ensure that all the information in this book is accurate. Due to differing conditions, equipment, tools, and individual skills, the publisher cannot be responsible for any injuries, losses, and other damages that may result from the use of the information in this book. Final determination of the suitability of any information, procedure or product for use contemplated by any user, and the manner of that use, is the sole responsibility of the user. This book is intended for informational purposes only.

The views, opinions and findings contained in this book are those of the author. The publishers, editors, reviewers and author assume no responsibility or liability for errors or any consequences arising from the use of the information contained herein. Registered names and trademarks, etc., used in this publication, even without specific indication thereof, are not to be considered unprotected by the law. Mention of trade names of commercial products does not constitute endorsement or recommendation for use by the publishers, editors or authors.

Publisher: Charles Spahr, Executive Director, The American Ceramic Society.

Art Book Program Manager: Bill Jones

eBook Manager: Steve Hecker

Manuscript Adviser: Fred Sweet

Graphic Design and Production: Melissa Bury, Bury Design, Westerville, Ohio

Frontispiece: Green ewer with iron chain and bail handle, wood grip, soda fired to cone 6, by Vince Pitelka. Photo by John Lucas, Tennessee Tech Photo Services.

For my wife, Judy.
Without her support and encouragement
this book could not have been written.

Acknowledgements

Immediately after the publication of my first book, The Extruder Book, I felt that I was probably done with large-scale writing projects. I was content to write the occasional instructional magazine article. As the years passed, however, I paid more attention to what people were accomplishing, artistically, with just a slab of clay as a common starting point. I was intrigued and felt like I wanted to see how much I could learn about this approach to handbuilding. I wanted to delve more deeply into what others were doing with it.

For images, I decided to rely exclusively on postings to the Clayart and Pottery Basics internet message boards to get the word out. I believed that, with the weekly volume of interaction I saw on these boards, they would be efficient, time-effective channels for promoting the new book and for soliciting contributions. I was amazed and gratified with the volume of responses I received. In just six weeks after posting my first request, I had received nearly 250 photographs from artists not just in North America but from as far away as Brazil and Argentina. By the twelfth week, I had well over 500.

Looking through the photos that arrived almost daily was a wonderful experience, though selecting which to include in book's gallery proved to be very difficult, given the caliber of the art and the quality of the photography.

So, with that, I wish to sincerely thank everyone who submitted photos and descriptions of their work and for recommending so many others to me. You and your work inspired me to persevere.

I also thank Bill Jones and the publishing staff at The American Ceramic Society. In 1998 they took a chance on me as an unpublished author and helped me realize my dream of writing a book. Since then we have forged a relationship that has yielded many opportunities for me to share what I learn as a student of ceramics culminating in this book.

Finally, I thank my friend Fred Sweet. He is, and always will be, my "go-to guy" for anything to do with ceramics. He guided me through the development of *The Extruder Book*, and when I told him I was planning to write a book about handbuilding, he offered to help without hesitation. Being able to draw on Fred's expertise as a potter and as a teacher was, and always will be, enormously valuable to me.

d.e.b.

Table of Contents

Acknowledgements vi
Chapter 1: Getting Started 1
Chapter 2: Setting Up Your Work Area 7
Chapter 3: Slab-Making Options 13
          U.S. Slab Roller Manufacturers 27
          Build Your Own Slab Roller 39
Chapter 4: Tools 49
Chapter 5: Demonstrations 65
          Demo 1: *Making a Three Tile Panel* 66
          Demo 2: *Carving a Foam Press Mold* 67
          Demo 3: *Using a Plaster Press Mold* 69
          Demo 4: *Using Props: Picture Frames* 71
          Demo 5: *Using a Slump Mold: Platter* 74
          Demo 6: *Using Slump Molds: Dishes* 76
          Demo 7: *Using Press Molds: Wall Pocket* 78
          Demo 8: *Making & Using Templates: Bowl* ... 80
          Demo 9: *Using Templates: Pitcher* 82
          Demo 10: *Using Drape Forms: Sculpture* 85
          Demo 11: *Joining Slabs: Lidded Box* 87
          Demo 12: *Joining Slabs: Mitered Box* 90
          Demo 13: *Using Forms: Tankard* 94
          Demo 14: *The One-Slab Pitcher* 97
          Demo 15: *Adding Texture: Free-form Bowl* ... 100
          Demo 16: *Using Drape Molds: Bowl* 103
Chapter 6: Drying, Firing and Glazing Considerations ... 109
Chapter 7: Gallery 117

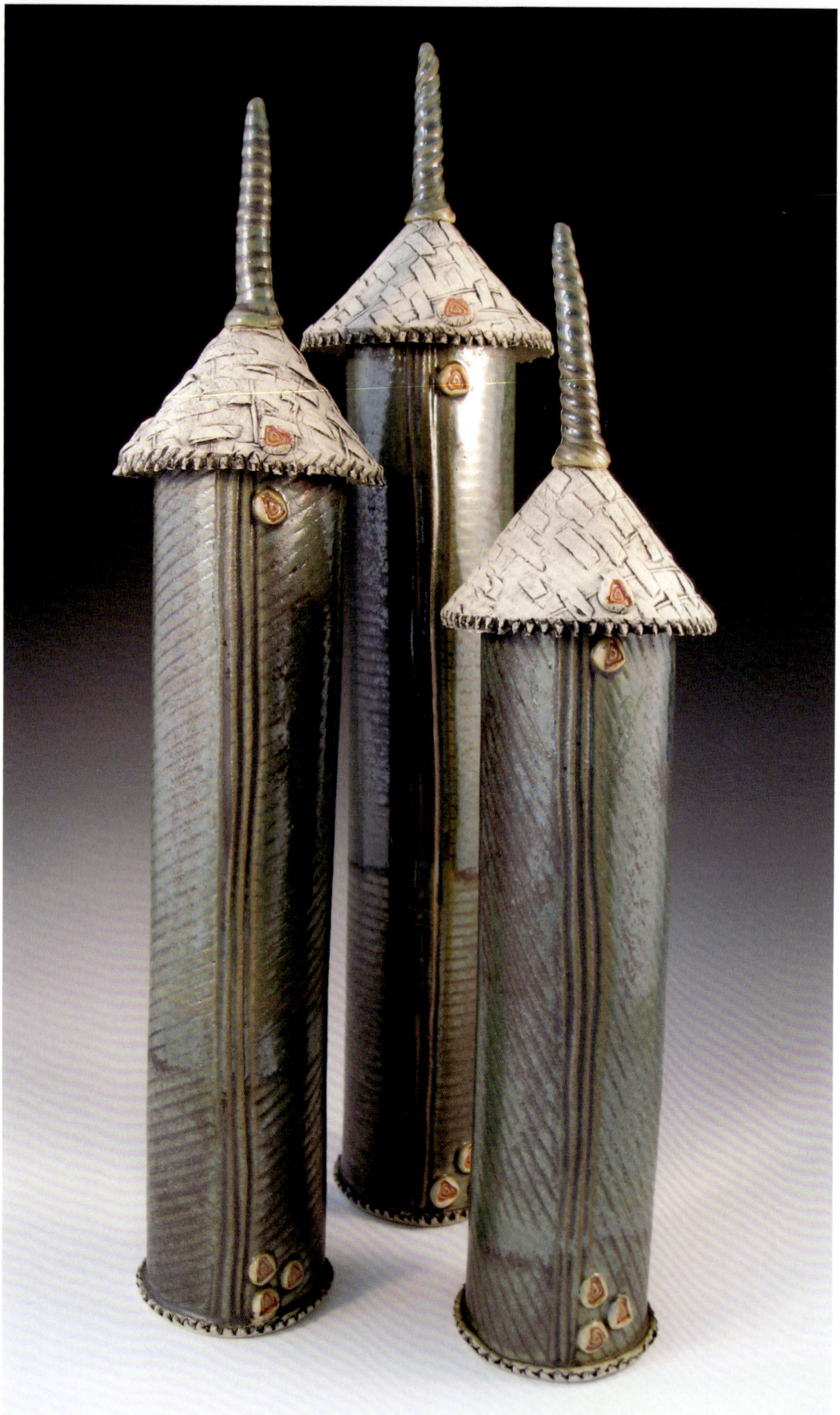

CHAPTER **1**

Getting Started

To derive the most enjoyment from working with any art medium it is important to familiarize yourself with it – to play with it awhile before attempting to do anything serious with it. So, that is where this book starts - by encouraging you to get acquainted with your clay by working it in your hands and learning its technical properties.

You need a comfortable, well-equipped place where you can nurture this budding relationship, so the next step is to show you how to set up your work space. From there, the many ways you can make slabs of clay are described, ranging from pressing them out by hand to using a variety of tools, including a slab roller.

The "Tools" chapter shows you the tools that can be used to express yourself in clay. Most who have some experience working with clay will agree that hunting for and collecting all of the smoothers, cutters, joiners, and especially the texture-makers, are the best parts of working with slabs of clay. This section also shows you how to make several very useful clay tools.

Once you have finished a piece, whether it is a simple tile or a multi-part sculpture, it has to be dried carefully before it goes into the kiln, so the book includes a section devoted to helping you avoid many of the pitfalls associated with firing your creations.

Next, through a series of step-by-step demonstrations, you are shown how to make a variety of functional and decorative objects. Each starts with a slab of clay and lists the tools & materials you will need before you start. These demonstrations illustrate how the tools are used and provide many opportunities for you to use

A collection of tools laid out on a 4x6-ft. table for easy access. This book describes how to make most of tools.

Towers, slab-built with coil finials, fired to cone 5 in oxidation, by Alice DeLisle.

your own tools and found objects. Also, many helpful tips are nested in the demonstrations so watch for them.

If you have accumulated everything described to this point, and if you have practiced the techniques, there are really only two ingredients to add. The first is imagination and you have to provide that. The second ingredient is inspiration and the book's photo gallery may supply a great deal of that. As you look through the gallery, bear in mind that all of the beautiful work you see started as slabs of clay and all of it was made using essentially the same tools and techniques that have been described for you.

Know Your Clay

Clay is a wonderful medium and the creative possibilities it offers are almost limitless. The variety of clay colors and textures can be bewildering, but, by gaining a basic understanding of clay characteristics, the process of selecting clay can be a very enjoyable part of the whole creative experience.

Clay suppliers provide both basic and highly specific details to aid in clay selection. All descriptions include the color and texture of the clay after it has been fired to maturity, and an estimation of how much the clay will shrink when it's fired. The more detailed descriptions offer recommended applications (e.g., tile-making, hand building, throwing), and include the clay body's absorption rate and a penetrometer number, which is an expression of the clay's density.

Some clay bodies are formulated to give them more stretch (plasticity) while others are mixed with sand, finely-milled brick or other clays to add strength, control shrinkage or reduce the risk of thermal shock.

Freshly made tiles from three different clays allowed to dry untouched.

The same three tiles after firing. Each has changed color, size and shape.

Selecting Clay

When held in your hand, pottery clay seems like such a simple material yet a great deal goes into it. Behind each commercially-prepared clay body, there's a great deal of careful testing. Once a clay body has been proven and it's gained market acceptance, the manufacturers strive for batch consistency so users can count on getting the same results with each bag of clay purchased.

At this point you may wonder which clay bodies are best for slab work. The simple answer is that slabs can be made from any clay, but different clay bodies yield different results for any given project.

To illustrate, three different clay bodies are rolled into slabs of the same thickness. One is earthenware clay, one is stoneware and one is porcelain. Each slab is cut into a square tile of the same size and allowed to dry completely, without further attention.

During drying, each tile shrank some and curled up slightly at the edges. During firing in the kiln the tiles, left and center, stayed fairly flat while the tile on the right curled even more. Each tile's color changed significantly and showed measurable shrinkage.

Earlier it was mentioned that clay manufacturers usually state the percentage of shrinkage to expect after a given clay is fired. This is very useful information for it helps you know how much larger you have to make something so it's the size you want after it's fired.

For example, if clay shrinks when it dries and is fired, how large does a plate have to be when you make it so it's twelve inches in diameter after you fire it? First, find out the stated shrinkage from the clay's specifications. For example, 13% (0.13) is typical for many stoneware clays. Subtract this from unity: 1.00 − 0.13 = 0.87. This is the shrinkage factor. Divide the shrinkage factor into the finished size you wish to obtain: 12 ÷ 0.87 = 13.79. So, the plate needs to be a little over 13¾ inches in diameter when you start to end up with a plate 12 inches in diameter when you finish. The formula applies to any dimension.

> **Absorption Rate:** Absorption rate is determined by carefully weighing a fully-fired piece of pottery then boiling the piece in water for two hours and re-weighing it. The dry weight is subtracted from the saturated weight and the difference is divided by the dry weight. The result is multiplied by 100 to get the absorption percentage.

Roll a fresh slab of clay that's ⅜- to ¾-inch thick, and cut a 2x10-inch tile from it. Use a metric ruler and lightly scribe a baseline at zero (0 cm).

Draw another line at 10 cm and another one at 20 cm.

Draw a perpendicular line between all three then dry the tile between two pieces of drywall to ensure it stays flat.

How to Determine Shrinkage

If, by chance, you don't know the stated percentage of shrinkage for your clay, here is a way to determine it yourself.

Determine the percentage of the clay's shrinkage by measuring the new length from the 0 cm line to the 10 cm line. Subtract the new length from 10 cm. Divide the difference by the original distance then multiply the result by 100. For example, if the new distance is 8.7 cm, then subtract that from 10 cm and you get 1.3 cm. Divide 1.3 by 10 and multiply by 100 to get a shrinkage rate of 13%. Verify this by measuring new length between the 0 cm mark and the 20 cm mark and making the same calculations.

By performing simple tests like these, you gain what might be considered a clinical, or scientific, familiarity with your clay. It's clearly important but it's meant to work hand in hand with the familiarity you develop by simply taking the clay out of the bag and playing with it. A potter planning to use the clay on a pottery wheel will wedge up a sample and see how the clay behaves while attempting to throw a pot. The clay tells them a great deal in just minutes. As a potter working with slabs, you should knead the clay then press out a small slab with it, all the while evaluating it in terms of its workability.

Getting Started

Preparing Clay

Most clay suppliers sell blocks of clays that are fresh, homogeneous and free of air pockets. Generally this clay is ready to use, right out of the bag. And, for most small- to medium-scale projects, cutting a chunk of clay off the block is the best way to start.

For clay to behave the way you want it to, it should be the same consistency throughout and wedging it with your hands is the best way to ensure you have clay that is free of hard spots or air pockets. This is especially the case when working with reconstituted or reclaimed clay that may have air trapped in it, or clay that may be drier in some places than others.

How do you know your clay is ready for use? As a rule, it's best to use clay that can easily be pinched and smeared between your thumb and forefinger. Rarely is there any advantage in starting a slab project with clay that requires extra exertion in wedging it.

When you purchased it, the clay was moist and ready to use. To keep it this way, remove as much air as possible from its bag before resealing it. Be sure there are no holes in the bag. For long-term storage, add a dampened cloth to the bag before sealing it.

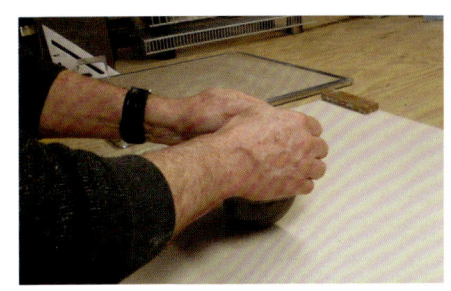

Grasp the clay and roll it back then press it forward into the wedging surface.

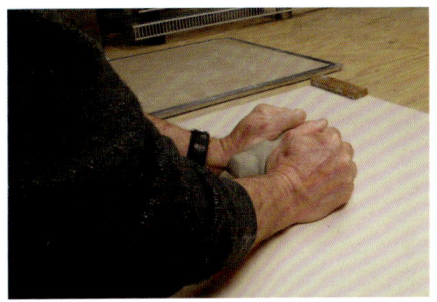

As the clay is folded over onto itself in a smooth motion, trapped air is pushed out.

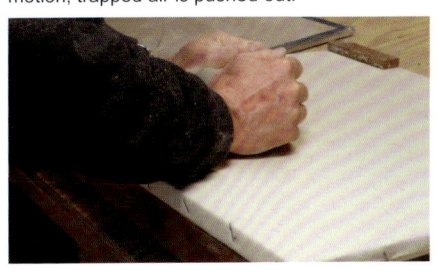

Keep the clay contained between the palms and rhythmically repeat the action.

The result is what is often referred to as the "bulldog" or "monkey face."

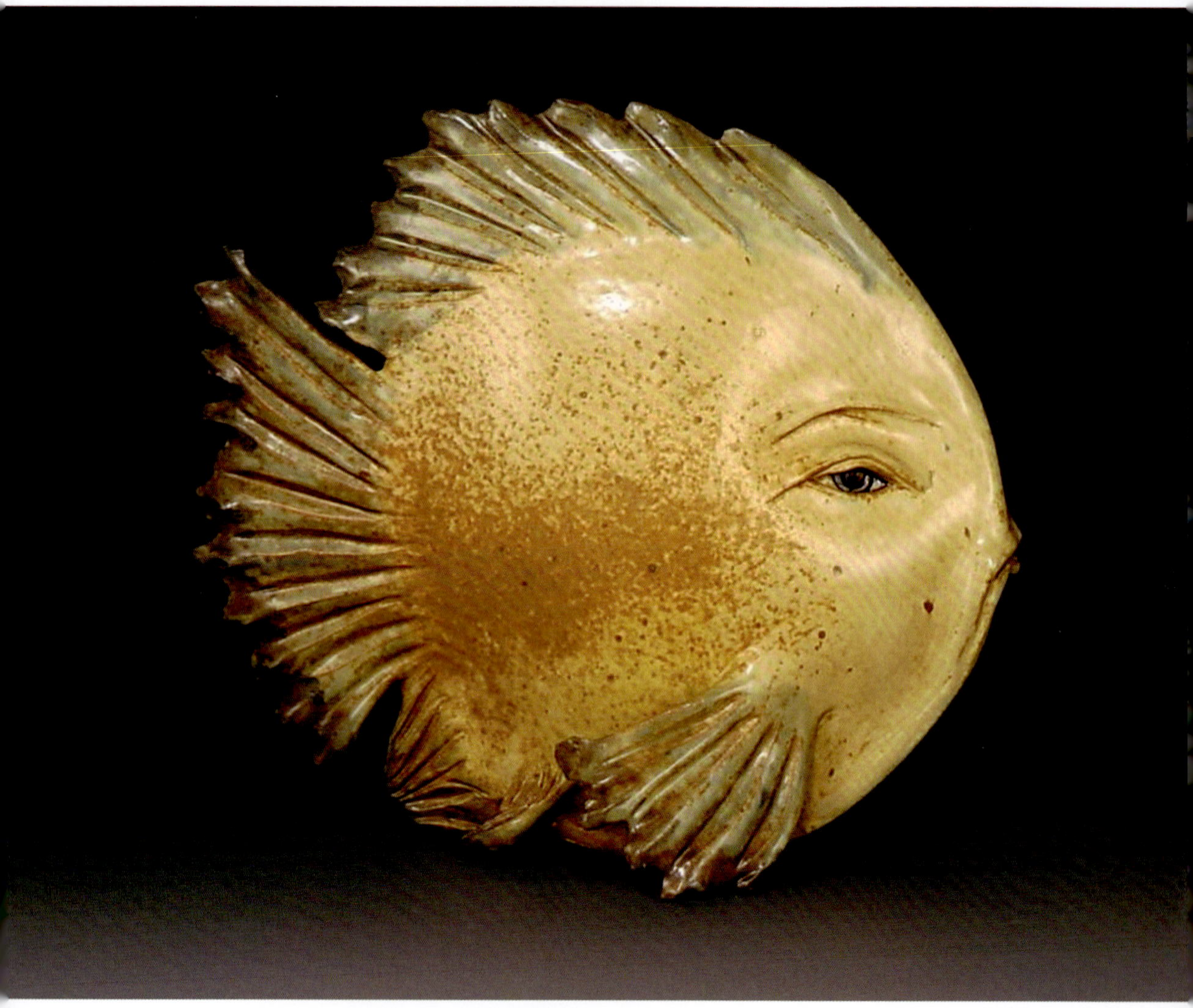

CHAPTER **2**

Setting Up Your Work Area

Now, let's talk about setting up the area where you will make your slabs and where you will work with them.

The table you use for wedging and making slabs needs to be very sturdy and capable of withstanding a great deal of pushing and slamming as you make your slabs. Tables with folding legs tend to wobble too much, but are okay for small-scale work.

Most dining tables are 29 to 30 inches tall. This is a suitable height for most people to do clay wedging and slab making. Shorter or taller people may wish to adjust the table height accordingly. The ideal worktable is at a height that allows you to exert downward and outward pressure on the clay while standing flat-footed with your knees slightly bent.

The ideal worktable also has enough peripheral area for tools to be laid out for quick selection. To be specific, the ideal worktable would be 30 inches high, 30 inches deep and 48 inches wide.

Adapting for Special Needs

The work area can be customized to accommodate a variety of special needs. For people who do their studio work from a wheelchair, the clay can be wedged on a board braced across the chair's armrests or at a table designed to allow the potter to move the wheelchair close enough, and at the correct height, for both wedging and construction work. Given the quantity and variety of tools used in slab work, one or more tool caddies, equipped with casters for easy positioning, make the small tools easily accessible.

This tool caddy, a yard sale find, keeps tools within easy reach whether working at a pottery wheel or from a wheelchair.

Fish, slab-built stoneware, by David Bellar.

Slab rolling tables can also be modified to suit people with special needs. Slab roller manufacturers offer shortened leg sets for their slab roller tables and slab rollers can be attached to homemade tables without altering the performance of the slab roller. The only consideration is that the crank or wheel has to be high enough for it to turn without any interference.

Larry Kruzan, owner of Lost Creek Pottery in Manito, Illinois, has his pottery studio set up so he can work safely and efficiently from his wheelchair. Larry uses a Bailey 32-inch DB series table equipped with a Bailey DRD electric roller for all of his slab work. His pug mill is located just four feet from the slab roller. He extrudes a two-foot pug of clay, takes it to the table and rolls it in a canvas sheet folded in half. Larry folds the rolled clay over one arm while it's still in the canvas then moves to the worktable just a couple of feet away. Once at the worktable, Larry peels back the canvas to reveal the slab. He sprinkles a plywood board with cornmeal and flips the canvas-backed slab onto it. He likes to prepare four or five slabs at a time in this fashion.

Larry Kruzan in his Manito, Illinois, studio.

The Work Surface

Here's a simple rule: The surface that you wedge your clay on and the surface on which you roll your slabs should be porous. Clay will stick to most metallic, plastic or painted surfaces. As Vince Pitelka points out in his book, *Clay: A Studio Handbook,* the choice of work surface is an important one. Plaster surfaces suck too much moisture. Wooden surfaces are fine, but if they are sealed, the clay easily sticks to them, and if not sealed they deteriorate rapidly. An ideal solution is to cover a table with heavy canvas.

If you don't have a table to dedicate to your slab work, you may find it more practical to make some slab boards. These should be sturdy and smooth and a good dimension is 24×24 inches. Several materials make good slab boards:

¾-inch Exterior plywood. The smooth surface, rigid strength, resistance to warping and durability make this a very good material for wedging and slab making. It can be used on both sides. It's comparatively expensive and requires a saw for cutting, but most home centers will cut it for free as a service. Additionally, plywood can be covered on both sides with heavy canvas, which adds an extra measure of absorbency to this type of slab board. One side of the board can be reserved for white clays and the other for red or brown clays.

½-inch Drywall. This has a smooth surface and can be used on both sides. When dry it offers good rigidity but, after becoming saturated with moisture from clay, it can become vulnerable to snapping; however, once dried, it's suitable for continued use. Drywall is also available in a ⅝ inch thickness that's better for slab work. It can absorb more moisture while maintaining its rigidity. Full 4×8-foot sheets are available at home improvement centers and one sheet can be easily cut into eight, very handy, 2-foot square slab boards using a utility knife; or you can buy pre-cut 2×2-foot pieces intended for wall repair. After cutting the drywall, use duct tape to seal all four edges to prevent the exposed plaster from flaking off. Masking tape isn't suitable because it dries out and peels away.

Cement board. Cement board is ideal for slab work, and it meets all of the key criteria—it's strong, rigid, and porous while being resistant

These slab boards, made from drywall, have stood up to years of use. Note that edges are sealed with duct tape.

to mold or fungus development, plus it's light-weight and easy to cut. HardieBacker® Cement Board (¼ in.) or the heavier (.42 in.) HardieBacker® 500 variety are common types.

> **Tip:** To help keep the slab board in place while working, add a cleat along one edge of each side of the board.

How to Make a Slab Board

MATERIALS
Exterior plywood
¾" x 24" x 24"
Canvas 36" x 72"
Lumber 1 x 2 x 24"
Wood screws (8)

TOOLS
Saw
Drill
Scissors
Screwdriver
Yardstick
Marking pen
Spring clamps (4)
Heavy-duty stapler
Carpenter's glue

1. Start with the 2-ft. square piece of plywood and smooth the edges with sandpaper. Cut four 5½-in. long cleats from 1x2 stock. Pre-drill two holes in each of the cleats and countersink them. Use 2 wood screws to attach each cleat after the board is covered with canvas.

2. Cut two 2½-in. canvas strips that are 24 in. long. Run a bead of glue along one plywood edge and spread it evenly. Press on the canvas, flip the board, and apply glue along the edge nearest you. Wrap the canvas and press it into the glue working quickly.

3. Attach spring clamps and allow glue to set. Attach the other strip of canvas to the opposite edge of the board in the same fashion. These strips cushion the end of the board to keep it from cutting through the canvas.

4. Cut out a piece of 25½x51-in. piece of canvas and attach it to the board using staples along the cushioned ends.

¾-inch Medium Density Fiberboard (MDF). This material can also be found at home improvement centers, and like plywood, must be cut to size. It's durable and has good rigid strength, but chips easily if dropped. It's not as porous as other materials listed.

As you get into slab work you will find that having a small collection of slab boards of different sizes and materials is very useful.

5. Wrap the canvas completely around the board and secure it with staples. Draw the canvas tight so you can fold under a cuff before stapling.

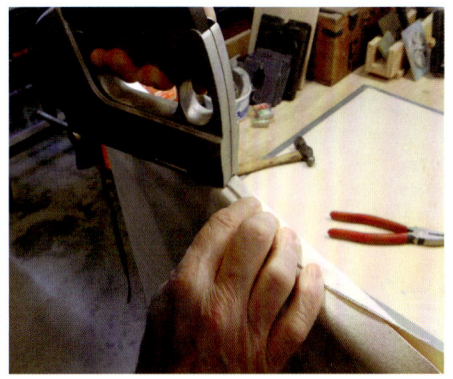

6. Finish the sides by first stapling down on edge of the fabric then folding over the other edge and stapling it into place. Tuck in and fold the extra canvas at each corner and staple securely.

7. Use one cleat to mark where the mounting holes go on the board. Drill the holes then attach the two cleats using wood screws. Flip the board and attach the other two cleats to the opposite end of the board.

8. The finished board. Note the placement of the cleats on the top and bottom.

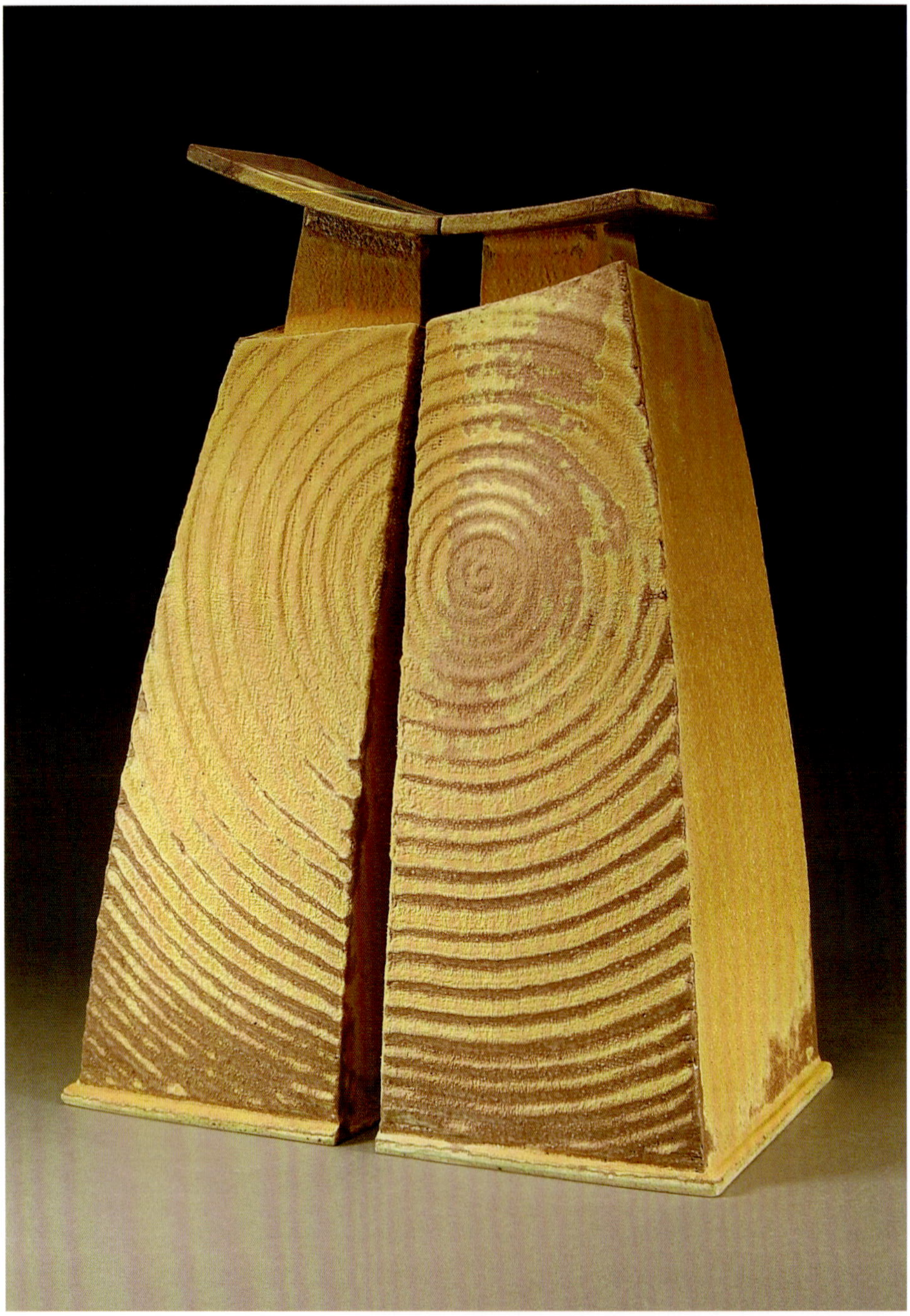

CHAPTER **3**

Slab-Making Options

Before you start to shape your clay into a slab, give some thought to how you will use your slab. Perhaps you're planning to cut the slab into tiles. Or, maybe you're planning to make a sign or a mask. In these cases, the clay can be rolled out on the slab board and left there while you work on it.

But, if you've made a slab from soft clay that is destined for placement in a mold or over a form, you need to be able to lift it and move it around without mangling it. So, what we need to establish, first off, is what you should have under your clay as you begin working with it.

Making Slabs Without Tools

While all the projects illustrated in this book involve using a rolling pin or slab roller, making slabs by hand warrants some discussion. For the best results when making slabs by hand, use soft clay. The key is to concentrate on pressing the clay out on a slab board with the heel of the hand, taking extra care to flatten the clay evenly in all directions. To get a flat surface, flip the clay onto a dry area of a slab board or cloth then continue to flatten the slab with the heel of your hand. Repeat this action several times until the slab is at the desired shape and thickness.

If you're working with stiffer clay, you can try to beat it into submission with the side of a rolling pin or a 4×4 block of wood. Work on one side then turn the clay over, rotate it 90° and beat it again. Continue this until the lump is adequately flattened.

Using Cutting Harps

Cutting harps are designed to cut slabs of even thickness from a block of fresh, soft clay. The home-made variety employs the use of a cutting wire or a length of heavy fishing line wrapped around two notched sticks. The sticks are held on each side of the clay block then drawn through it in one smooth motion. The wire is moved down a notch and another cut is made. With practice, consistent results can be achieved. There are also a few models of clay harps offered by pottery suppliers.

Towers 2, porcelainous stoneware fired to cone 04 in an electric kiln, by James Freeman, ht: 14 in.

From a Slab of Clay

Use a miter saw to cut evenly spaced notches into two sticks.

Draw the wire through the clay with the wire tight across the notches.

Clay harps are available from ceramic suppliers.

A twisted wire can be drawn through clay straight or side-to-side to vary the pattern.

After cutting the slabs with the clay harp, use them as is or roll them out to reduce the thickness. You can also "stitch" them together to make larger slabs by simply overlapping the edges and blending the two surfaces together using your finger or thumb. Turn the slab over and repeat the blending process. It's important that all seams are melded well to avoid cracking later. Use a small roller or a rib to smooth the assembled slab.

Cutting Slabs Freehand

In slab making there is a great deal of emphasis given to starting with slabs that are evenly stretched and of uniform thickness. But there are a number of opportunities to employ slabs cut freehand from a block of clay then further manipulated. The technique illustrated above involves using a twisted wire available at ceramic supply stores.

Slab-Making Options

Using Rolling Pins

While rolling pins are made from a variety of materials, those made from unfinished wood are ideally suited for use in making clay slabs. Clay doesn't stick to the roller's porous wood so it stays flat on the slab board while being rolled. The rolling pin is just the first of many tools that got their

Scraps of wood molding cut to length make ideal "roller rests."

start in the kitchen but found their way into the pottery studio. There are three basic types of rolling pin that find their way into the pottery studio: the basic cylinder, the cylinder with ball-shaped knobs in the ends and the type of pin that has a handle attached to each end of a rod that runs through the center of the cylinder. A fourth type, the tapered, or French pastry pin, also finds some limited use. John W. Reed is credited with the invention of the third type of rolling pin in 1864. Little did he know then that his invention would find

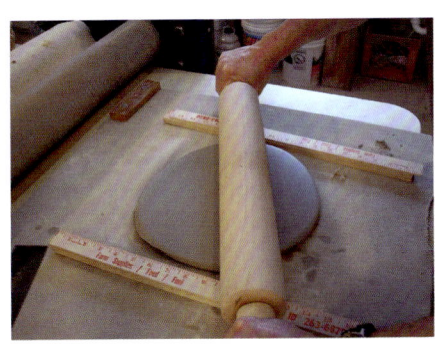

To roll a slab, place clay between stacks of flat sticks made from lath or wooden yardsticks.

Lift, rotate 90° and flip the clay over after each pass.

Remove two sticks and repeat.

Silicone rings of various thicknesses from a kitchen supply store slip onto a rolling pin.

Support Your Local Slab

Before you start to shape your clay into a slab, give some thought to how you will use your slab. If you're planning to cut it into tiles or decide to make a sign or a mask, you can just roll the clay out on the slab board and leave it there while you work on it. But, if you've made a soft clay slab to place in a mold or over a form, you'll need to be able to lift and move it around without mangling it. So, what we need to establish is what you should have under your clay as you begin working with it.

- Use canvas, sturdy fabric or even heavyweight paper as a cradle. If you roll your slab with something underneath, you can easily lift it and avoid touching it at all as you move and handle it. Do not roll clay directly onto a surface where it can be difficult to lift off. With the clay on fabric or paper, it can be easily lifted and flipped. To flip a slab, lay another piece of cloth or paper on top of it then flip it in one continuous motion.

- If your clay rests on canvas only and isn't supported by a board, place a piece of drywall on top of the slab, then lift one end of the canvas and hold it tightly against the end of the board. As you flip the slab over, it will flex with the canvas. Try to bend and stretch it as little as possible.

- Roll one end of the slab onto a rolling pin, or other porous cylinder, then lift the slab. The rolling pin keeps the slab smooth and free from finger impressions while transporting it.

- Lifting a thin clay slab with your fingers can stretch, even tear, the clay. Instead, grasp each end of the slab with two flat sticks, one on the front of the slab and one behind it on the back of the slab. Rulers or paint stirring sticks are suitable for this. Grasping each pair of sticks, lift the slab and quickly transfer it.

Roll one end of the slab onto a rolling pin then lift to keep it smooth during transporting.

To lift a slab without stretching or tearing it, hold each end of it between two flat sticks.

A Do-It-Yourself Rolling Pin

You can make a heavy, durable, non-stick rolling pin by filling a 4-in. diameter cardboard tube with potter's plaster. Carpeting is rolled on tubes of this size. Stand the tube in a pan, on a tile, or directly on a cement floor then seal around the bottom with clay. Mix enough plaster to ensure you can fill the tube completely. As you pour in the plaster, tap the side of the tube with a block of wood or a small mallet to help air bubbles rise to the top and escape. Once the plaster has set up, peel the paper off. Spiral marks can be sanded off. This method yields a 15 to 20 pound roller. Use a "roller rest" made from wooden molding to keep it from rolling off the table.

Pour plaster into a cardboard tube to create a rolling pin. Tap the tube after pouring to release bubbles from the plaster. Remove the cardboard after the plaster sets.

lasting favor beyond the bakery; not just with the wives of truant husbands, but with those of us who are devoted slab-builders.

To make a basic slab of even thickness and compression, press out the clay evenly by hand. When it's just over an inch thick, place a stack of four flat sticks on either side and roll from the center outward. Lift the clay off of the canvas, turn it 90° and flip it over. Remove one stick from each stack and roll again from the center to the edges. Repeat and remove two more sticks.

As an alternative to the stacked stick technique, some potters have attached door knobs or wooden disks to the ends of rolling pins. These set the gap between the roller and the work surface and help make slabs of uniform thickness. Yet another way to get slabs of even thickness is to slide a pair of silicone rings onto the rolling pin. These are sold in kitchen supply stores and come in sets of four different thicknesses: $^1/_{16}$, $^1/_8$, ¼ and ½ inch. They will fit 2¼–3 in. diameter rolling pins. For a snugger fit, two or three layers of painter's tape can be added to each end of the roller (as shown).

Using a Pottery Wheel

The pottery wheel presents two ways to make slabs—horizontally and vertically. The horizontal approach might be the least-used, but wheel-thrown slabs have some unique properties and there are those who actually prefer them.

Making Horizontal Wheel-Thrown Slabs

A comparatively thick slab of clay is spread out on the wheel head then allowed to firm slightly. After drawing a cutting wire across the bottom on the slab, it's lifted from the wheelhead and laid on the work surface. As expected, lifting and transporting the clay to the work surface deforms the circular slab; but this can be minimized by first underscoring the periphery of the slab with a trimming tool then rolling it up and onto a rolling pin or sturdy cardboard tube.

Optionally, the wheel-thrown slab can be allowed to firm up on the wheel head after cutting. This firmer slab loses some of its workability but it can be lifted and transported with less deformity. Clay slabs thrown on plastic or wood-composite bats can be removed from the wheel head and placed next to the work surface before removal. Bats made from plaster can be especially useful since plaster wicks moisture from the underside of the slab while it's going through controlled drying on the top surface. As the clay firms up and starts to shrink, it releases from the plaster bat with little or no effort.

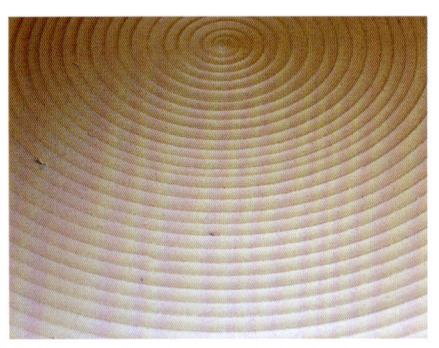

A slab can be made on a potter's wheel and removed while pliable or when leather-hard depending on your project.

A spiral texture like this is almost impossible using any other method than throwing.

Slab-Making Options

The sides and top of this small box were cut from the slab shown above.

At 12 in. high and 9½ in. dia. this thrown cylinder yields nearly 360 sq. in. of slab.

It's important to develop a technique where you can apply even compression of the clay across the surface, from center to edge. Doing so makes for a stronger slab that's more likely to keep its shape. What makes wheel thrown slabs distinctive are the concentric and spiral textures that can be added to them. Running a finger across the clay as the wheel spins can make a simple, spiral ridge. More detailed textures can be applied using roulettes, stamps or any combination of them. Once the slab is decorated and released from its bat, it can be cut into shapes or wrapped around a form.

Making Vertical Wheel-Thrown Slabs

Simply put, this slab is a pot with a vertical wall and no base. This cylinder is allowed to firm up while it is on the wheel head then it is cut away and moved to the work surface. The cylinder can be cut down the side into several pieces then reassembled or, with just one cut down the side, it can be opened and laid flat on the work surface. It's interesting to note that a wheel-thrown cylinder, with a diameter of fifteen inches, yields a slab almost four feet long.

Extrude cylinders of uniform thickness using soft, well-wedged clay pushed through a die using constant pressure.

Use a fettling knife or needle tool to open the cylinder.

Using an Extruder and Dies

A clay extruder and a set of dies present a number of possibilities for making slabs. When clay passes through a die it's evenly compressed and this makes for better-behaved slabs. While several die shapes are suitable for slab making, two are particularly useful—the hollow cylinder, circular or elliptical, and one often referred to as a "tile die."

Clay pushed through a hollow cylinder die yields a tube that, like the cylinder thrown on a pottery wheel, can be handled a number of ways. It can be cut down the side, opened and rolled flat into a slab, or it can be cut into several pieces.

Roll out the slab using a rolling pin scaled to work you're performing.

A Bailey 4x6 tile barrel extrudes tiles up to 6 inches wide and the adapter extrudes tiles up to 14 inches wide.

Extruder Tips
To get the best with extruders and dies, here are some tips.
- Use soft clay that's even in consistency and free of air pockets.
- Apply slow, constant pressure on the extruder handle while extruding.
- Support large extrusions from the base to minimize stretch.
- Guide the extrusion with the free hand, front to back and side to side.
- Have an assistant operate the handle while you guide the extrusion.
- Prepare your work surface for placement of the extrusion.
- Locate the work surface close to the extruder to minimize distortion in transit.

Tile dies produce flat sheets of clay and are available in various widths from pottery equipment suppliers or they can be custom made. Extrusions made with a tile die can be left very long and used for large-scale projects, or they can be cut to size and manipulated in a variety of ways.

Using a Slab Roller

Slab rollers have been commercially manufactured and available for studio work for more than forty years. They're designed to do one thing—turn a mound of clay into a beautiful, enticing, creativity-inspiring slab of clay. While there are no steadfast rules to follow when using a slab roller to make a slab of clay, there are some routine steps that can make things go easier and help you get the results you want.

Long extrusions can be textured then cut into uniform lengths to make several tiles of the same thickness and width

Before You Start

If using a slab roller is new to you, take time to familiarize yourself with its basic operation before attempting to work with clay.

- Turn the crank or wheel and observe the rotation of the roller or rolls. The mechanism should operate smoothly in either direction.
- The handle, or wheel, should be firmly attached and it should turn freely with minimum effort.
- The table shouldn't wobble, so check all bolts in the frame and legs if it does.
- Canvas sheets should be free of loose threads, and shim boards should be smooth on both sides.
- Rollers should be free of caked-on clay that can interfere with their ability to perform. Caution: Brushing dry clay from the rollers can be dusty work, so remove dry clay with a damp sponge.
- If a copy is available, read any manufacturer instructions.

Slab Roller Sheets

Before you can actually use a slab roller, you need to understand that clay isn't supposed to go through the rollers by itself. Typically it goes through the rollers sandwiched between two pieces of canvas, or inside a single piece of canvas that's been folded in half. Canvas is used most often because its texture can be gripped by the rollers and pulled through with minimum slippage.

But the problem with canvas is that it imparts a characteristic texture to the slab. If this is not desired, it can be removed by lightly misting the surface of the slab with water then drawing a paint trim guide across it several times. Other fabrics can be used between the canvas and clay to give the slab a smoother surface:

> **CAUTION:** Dry canvas sheets used with slab rollers can release unhealthy dust into the studio air. Avoid shaking the canvas and, to help control the dust, lightly spray both sides of the canvas with water before rolling clay.

Ticking. This is a heavy cotton fabric similar in weight to denim, which is traditionally used to cover pillows and as an upholstery fabric.

Suede cloth. This 100% polyester has a velvet-like nap finish.

Thermal drapery lining. This cloth has a suede-like surface and does not stretch.

Denim. In terms of texture, denim falls in between canvas and the other fabrics listed. Denim is very durable and, like canvas, stands up to heavy usage.

Sheets or old pillow cases that have been cut down the sides, make a nice, smooth slab roller sheet. Control fraying fabric by serging all four edges.

What else? Many other flat materials such as flocked wallpaper, construction paper, heavy cardboard and chipboard can be sent through the slab roller with your clay. While it's fun to experiment, bear in mind that slab rollers are not indestructible. Avoid sending anything through that would overtax the mechanism.

Rolling the Slab

Though the larger slab roller assemblies are sturdy enough to handle a large mass of stiff clay at the narrowest setting in one pass, this isn't the best way to roll your slabs. All of your exertion and the strain on the mechanism aren't necessary. The best technique is to develop the shape and thickness of your slab incrementally by thinning it gradually in three or four passes. Set the starting gap between the rollers to three or four times the desired thickness of

This Bailey DRD/II easily handles large masses of clay, but you'll get better results by thinning slabs in three or four passes.

the slab then widen the gap a bit more to allow for the thickness of anything else that's passing through with the clay. For example, if you want a slab that's ¼-in. thick, set the gap to approximately 1 inch and start with a clay mass that is 25% to 50% thicker than the starting gap, say, 1¼ to 1½ inches thick. Next, taper the leading edge of the clay mass by tapping it with your fist then lay the cover material over the clay and feed it forward until the clay nudges up to the roller.

Turn the handle or wheel slowly as the clay is drawn under the roller and out the other side. Now, uncover the clay, lift and turn it 90°, if you want a slab that it as wide as it is long, otherwise, leave it in place.

If you're working with heavily textured material like duck canvas, the clay can work deeply into the weave. To help the clay move as it goes under the roller, first lift the slab from the cloth then let it down to release it and continue rolling. Next, adjust the roller gap so it's about 25% narrower than the starting gap, then pass the clay and its cover material through again. Repeat the procedure a couple more times until the desired thickness is attained.

The same sort of technique is followed for slab rollers that rely on the stacking of shim boards for gap adjustment. The first pass is made over the clay as it rests on a sheet of material that is resting directly on the bed. The clay can be turned then the first shim board is slid beneath the bottom sheet. The clay is rolled over again and the procedure is repeated.

Note: Whether or not to flip the clay slab over with each pass is a matter that is open to dispute. Some insist that it's the only way to develop a slab that won't warp. Others hold that the flipping isn't necessary in slab roller assemblies having two rollers.

Troubleshooting

It may be largely a matter of trial and error. In most cases the aim is to develop a clay slab that is evenly stretched in all directions. There certainly are exceptions; especially where the clay slab is going to be manipulated a great deal after it comes off the roller table. Improper rolling, whether by hand or with a machine, can ruin the finished product. As Vince Pitelka points out, if you roll in only one direction, you are setting up a grain structure similar that of a wooden board. The slab will shrink more across the width than the length. If you assemble a form from unevenly stretched slabs, the form will likely pull itself apart because of different shrinkage in the drying and/or firing.

Choosing a Slab Roller

You can buy a slab roller alone or you can buy the roller in a complete package with legs and a table. Some have simple hand cranks while others are equipped with large "wagon wheels." Some have one roller, others two, and they come in a variety of widths—from 16 inches up to 40 inches—and the tables are anywhere from a 18 inches long up to 7 feet. Some slab rollers are designed for portability while the rest are floor models that can take up a lot of space in a small studio. Some are light-duty while others are "industrial-grade" and built to work under heavy demand, day in and day out. Prices range from under $200 to more than $2,000.

So, which slab roller is right for you? Let's take the classic investigative approach and ask: Who? What? Where? and When? We'll drop Why? but we'll add How much?

WHO is going to use the slab roller?

Answering this may help you determine whether or not you'll need a model designed to sustain heavy use. Some light-duty models carry a limited warranty explicitly stating that they're not intended for commercial or institutional use. If several people are going to use the slab roller, get input from them as to what they want to do with it and how often they plan to use it. Also, do you or anyone else have any physical limitations that might interfere with your ability to operate the slab roller? If so, "try before you buy."

WHAT do you plan to do with the slab roller?

You're going to roll out slabs of clay, of course, but what will be the width and length of most of your slabs? Will most of your slabs be around one square foot and ¼-in. thick, or will you be doing larger projects that require slabs two to three feet wide, several feet long and a ½-in. thick? In slab rollers, bigger isn't always better. If it looks like you're going to do mostly small-scale projects, requiring slabs no wider than sixteen inches, then a portable or a light-duty floor model may fill the bill.

WHERE will the roller be used?

In many studios, space is precious and careful planning is required when adding a floor-model slab roller. It's sort of like trying to put a billiard table in a guest room—it may fit but you really can't use it because you need room for more than just the table. Ideally, you should have an area in the studio equivalent to the dimensions of the slab roller's table plus an additional two feet of free area all around. However, most floor models on the market can be located against a wall and still conveniently operated, while some come with locking casters, or you can add casters to an existing roller. Bear in mind that slab rollers equipped with tables also make excellent working surfaces for other studio projects. You may find that a table or bench you're using now can be replaced with a slab roller without losing a lot of workspace. If you need to travel with your slab roller, there are six portable models available.

WHEN *will the slab roller be used?*
This also relates to the amount of use the slab roller will receive. Will the slab roller be used on a daily basis or just occasionally? The answer here will help you determine if you should invest in one of the heavy-duty models, which are often equipped with ultra-strong gearing and 4-in. rollers. Look for lifetime warranties here.

HOW MUCH *are you planning to spend?*
While this may be your dealer's opening question, it may not necessarily be the first question to ask yourself. By evaluating your needs before your budget, you can do a better job of getting the right slab roller that will suit your needs. With slab rollers, bigger isn't always better.

U.S. Slab Roller Manufacturers

Among the U.S. companies that manufacture and/or distribute slab rollers, the slab roller product lines of the three largest are profiled below. Each company offers a wide variety of models that range from small portables to full-size models with their own stand-alone tables. As of this printing, North Star Equipment manufactures eight slab rollers, Amaco five, and Bailey Pottery Equipment thirteen. Laguna Clay Company expanded its pottery equipment line to include The Bellar Roller, a vertical slab roller. There are a lot of slab rollers to choose from and a number of options to consider.

> **Note:** The intent here is to provide detailed, objective information including product specifications, assembly requirements, optional equipment and operation. The manufacturers provided all product details.

North Star Equipment, Inc. (Cheney, WA)
www.northstarequipment.com

Standard and Super Series
North Star slab rollers are made in two series: The Standard series recommended for use by hobby potters and students, and the Super series suited for industrial, institutional and production settings. All models employ a two-roller mechanism where the clay is drawn through and flattened as the crank or wheel is turned. On Standard models, the crank is directly connected to the bottom roller, or *roll*; and Super models have a large wagon wheel connected to a gear that meshes with another gear connected to the bottom roller.

    The rollers have a small diamond pattern machined directly into the metal (called *knurling*). This knurling helps the roller assembly grip the canvas. The bottom roll is turned by the handle, but cannot move vertically. As it turns, it drives the top roll through a train of gears. The upper roll both rotates and can be adjusted vertically. The two rolls turning together pull the slab through. The height of the top roll is adjusted with a knob on each end of the roller assembly. The gap between the rollers can be any thickness from paper-thin to more than 2 inches. A reference scale allows setting and repeating openings to within $1/100$ of an inch. A variety of texturing materials and objects can be passed through the machine along with the clay. Slabs can be rolled in either direction on all North Star machines.

The bodies and rolls in North Star's slab roller assemblies are made of cast and machined, high-strength special alloy aluminum. Gears are made of steel, bushings are nylon and the remaining parts (except plastic gear covers and knobs) are machined steel. Table frames are 14-gauge steel, and tabletops made from moisture-resistant Medex with a melamine surface. Metal surfaces are zinc plated or coated with a durable powder coat finish.

Virtually no maintenance is required, and the simplicity of the design ensures that any repair, ever needed, will be quick and easy. Standard models are 18 or 24 inches wide, although a special-order 30-in. wide roller is available. All Standard models have rollers that are 2½ inches in diameter. The tables are 48 inches long with the roller assembly in the center. The handle drives the bottom roll directly. The Super models are much heavier, the tables are 72 inches long, and the rolls are 4 inches in diameter. There is a 4.33:1 steel gear reduction between handle and roll. Supers are made in 24-, 30- and 36-in. widths, and are equipped with the exclusive Wagon Wheel handle.

The North Star Standard 24 Package equipped with optional end wing (left), bucket wing (right) and bottom shelf kit.

Optional Equipment

Bottom Shelf

A bottom shelf is available for installation on Standard series tables. It's made of ¾-in. Medex with a high-pressure melamine overlay in two sections, and is supported by steel rails all around. The shelf requires some drilling, but no disassembly of the table is required. A precision drilling template and all hardware is furnished. The shelf can support 600 pounds.

End Wings

End wings, or *extensions*, fold out and lock horizontally during use, and fold down against the legs when not in use. Wings measure ¾×24×24 inches and can support up to 100 pounds each.

Bucket Wing

This specialized wing has an opening that accommodates a 5-gallon plastic bucket or the included 15-in. plastic throwing bat that fills the opening and makes a smooth, level top when a bucket is not being used.

North Star PortaRoller and Polaris CT-500

The PortaRoller combines North Star's 18-in. Standard slab roller with a specially designed set of Table Toppers. The PortaRoller was designed for ceramic art teachers who move from classroom to classroom, and for studio potters who need a fully-functional slab roller but have limited space. The PortaRoller is constructed from the same materials and operates the same way as their Standard slab rollers. The two Table Toppers are made of moisture-resistant Medex with a melamine surface. The PortaRoller's crank handle is

Note: North Star roller assemblies are shipped fully assembled. Tables and optional equipment require assembly.

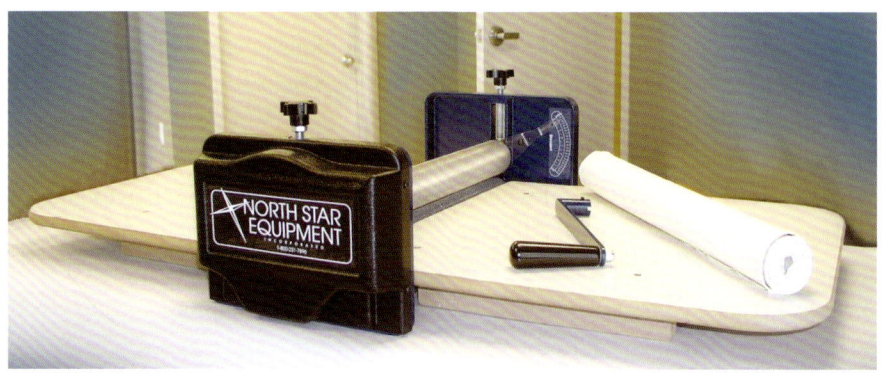

North Star offers portable slab rollers including the 18-in. PortaRoller and the 24-in. Polaris CT-500. A portable slab roller is perfect for demonstrators and artists with limited studio space.

removable and it fits into two clips under one of the Table Toppers. Combine the North Star 24-in. Standard slab roller with a specially designed set of Table Toppers and you have the North Star Polaris CT-500, a larger version of the PortaRoller. This larger model, while heavier, affords the teacher or studio potter a portable slab roller capable of making wider and longer slabs than the PortaRoller.

Bailey Pottery Equipment Corporation (Kingston, NY)
www.baileypotteryequipment.com

Bailey DRD/II Slab Roller

Bailey offers two table options for its DRD/II Slab Roller. The larger 6-ft. long table has a full 48-in. long area on the right side of the machine for work on the finished slab. A shorter 4-ft. long table has a 32-in. work area. All Bailey tables, with the exception of the DB and Mini series, have a smaller feed counter on the left side of the roller assembly and a larger area on the right side for the finished slab. The counters are made of Melamine.

The Bailey DRD/II Outfit shown with optional 34-in. diameter wheel and casters.

    Bailey roller assemblies are shipped fully assembled. Tables require assembly.

    Bailey employs an all-steel gear reduction system designed for strength, durability and ease of operation. It is offered on the 30-in. and the 24-in. gear reduced models.

    Bailey slab rollers are designed with a simultaneous height adjustment feature where one knob is turned to adjust the gap between the rolls. A height scale, from $1/32$ to $1\frac{1}{2}$ inches is installed.

    The DRD/II series comes with a canvas sheet and a 4-spoke handle. An optional 34-in. diameter round wheel is available. This large wheel gives ample leverage to make rolling easier and more fluid. A reverse-threaded adapter comes standard on both the 4-spoke and round handle of all gear-reduced machines. This adapter was designed especially for classrooms and group studios to prevent damage to the machine.

Bailey Basic 30-D Slab Roller

The Bailey Basic 30-D Slab Roller is an economically-priced model designed for use by serious hobbyist potters. This machine is intended to offer all the professional features for potters who require a low-volume output of slabs. According to the manufacturer, when used with this expectation, the machine will last a lifetime.

The Basic 30-D's rollers are 30 inches wide and 2½ inches in diameter and made of knurled aluminum. A 23-in. diameter round wheel connects directly to the shaft of the bottom roller and supplies the leverage to roll the clay. When feeding clay through the Bailey Basic 30D, it's recommended you use plastic, easily-wedged clay to feed through the machine. The thickness of the finished slab ($1/16$ to 2 inches) determines the height of the feed clay. The gap between the rolls is adjusted at one side of the machine and an inch scale is provided for measurement.

The Bailey Basic 30 roller can be mounted to the optional Bailey bi-level 52-in. table. This overall table length is 52 inches and it comes with casters so it can be moved around the work area. On the Bi-Level, the slab roller is off to one side, and the area the rolled slab moves onto is 32 inches long. The table

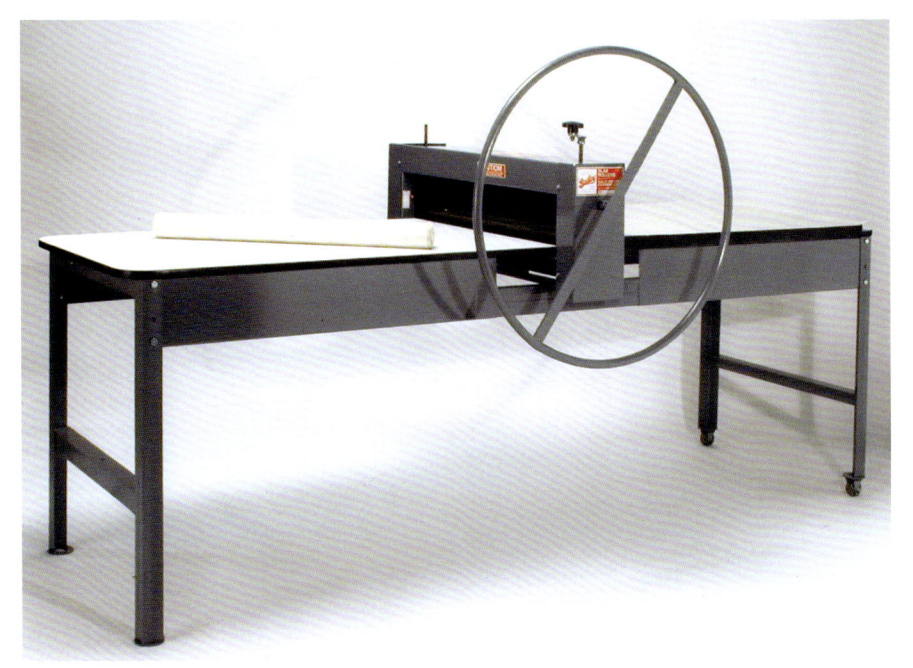

Bailey DB (Drive Board) Series rollers are available in 30- and 40-in. widths, manual or electric.

has a lower-level feed counter so more of the bottom roller is exposed, which provides better gripping of the canvas and clay and aids compression of the clay for a stronger slab. The slab counter (i.e., the table top) is higher than the lower-level feed counter; almost level with the top of the bottom roller. This allows the slab to roll out longer with greater variety of thicknesses and without bunching.

Bailey offers its table counters (or tabletops) as options. You can purchase a complete table or buy only the steel frame and make your own counters from plywood or particleboard. One counter is 30×32 inches and the other is 30×16 inches.

The Bailey Basic 30 can also be mounted on any table using home-made "ramp-style counters." The intake ramp is placed at the front of the roller and the output ramp is placed at the back. Neither ramp requires permanent fastening. By removing the ramps and roller the table can be used for other functions. Bailey provides the dimensions for making the ramp-style counters or they can be purchased pre-made.

The Bailey DRD 30 has 4-in. diameter rollers and additional sprocket and chain reduction. A 34-in. diameter wheel is standard. Shown on optional table equipped with casters

The Bailey Basic 30-D comes standard with a 23-in. diameter wheel and canvas. Shown with optional table mount counters. A complete mobile table for the Basic 30-D model is also available.

Slab-Making Options

Bailey Mini 22-in. Table Roller

The Bailey Mini 22-in. Table Roller is a model that utilizes the same "dual roller drive" process as Bailey's larger models. With it you can make slabs up to 22 inches wide and 24 inches long. By using longer shim boards, longer slabs can be made. The slab thickness can be adjusted from 1/8 inch to 3/4 inches in 1/8-in. increments. By adding shim material, even thinner slabs can be rolled. The rolls are textured to facilitate passage of the clay, and a 15-in. hand crank is used to operate the roller assembly. The design is a combination slab roller and table mount in one machine.

Every Table Roller is supplied with a set of Masonite shims and a slab sheet. Side guides keep the Masonite shims on center as they pass through the rollers. An optional Mini Leg Set converts the Table Roller into a freestanding table. Some assembly is required for both roller and table.

Bailey 16-in. Mini-Might Table Top Roller

The Bailey 16-in. Table Top Mini-Might is a portable slab roller designed for both the professional and the hobbyist. It has rubber feet for stability, and can produce up to a 16×18-in. slab using the same interval thickness system as the Mini Might 22. Some assembly is required.

The Bailey Mini 22-in. Table Roller (shown with optional legs) and the Bailey 16-in. Mini-Might Table Top Roller. Bailey Pottery originated the portable slab roller design.

Amaco/Brent (Indianapolis, IN)
www.amaco.com

Amaco manufactures the Brent line of slab rollers. Amaco/Brent's larger slab roller tables employ a design where the clay is laid on the table bed then a cable-driven roller moves across it as the handle or wheel is turned. The slab is made thinner by adding one or more shim boards then passing the roller over the clay again. All SR models are designed as a single roller opposing four casters for constant pressure.

Brent SR-36
The Brent SR-36 is a large floor model that can produce up to 36×52-in. slabs with a maximum thickness of $^7/_8$ inch. The SR-36 comes with one ¼-in. and one $^1/_8$-in. plain shims and one ¼-in. canvas covered shim. Because the amount of clay and the mechanical pressure that is produced rolling a large slab, the middle of the SR-36's bed may bow slightly, creating a slab that's thinner on the sides. This variation is more evident when attempting to roll thinner slabs (⅜- to ½-in.). The effect is not quite as evident on thicker slabs, thus this slab roller is best suited for large-scale projects. Amaco recommends its smaller models for making thinner slabs of consistent thickness.

The Brent SR-36 made by Amaco/Brent is designed for large-scale projects. The Brent roller moves over the clay using a cable system instead of the clay moving through the geared rollers.

Slab-Making Options

Brent SR-20 and Brent SR-14

The Brent SR-20 and SR-14 are smaller versions of the SR-36. The Brent SR-20 is a mid-sized floor model that can produce up to 20×52-in. slabs. They include one ¼-in. canvas covered shim and one ⅛-in. plain shim, and can produce a slab up to 1½ inches thick. The Brent SR-14 table model can also be used as a floor model by adding an optional leg set, and is capable of producing a 14×36-in. slab up to 1¾ inches thick.

The Brent SR-20 (above) and the Brent SR-14 (below). The Brent SR-14 can be placed on an existing tabletop but also can be outfitted with an optional leg set (shown).

Brent SRC

The Brent SRC is a portable slab roller designed for small projects, and capable of producing up to 21×40-in. slabs. It is not suitable for heavy-volume production work or for schools. It can be used on a table or as a floor model with an optional leg set and has a patented cable drive system with opposing rollers that produces even pressure along the bed. The SRC comes with one ¼-in. shim with canvas, four ¼-in. plain shims and one ⅛-in. plain shim.

Brent Mini SRC

Portable, yet extremely sturdy, this slab roller is compact enough to fit on a table while rolling out slabs up to 14 inches wide and 15 inches long. Maximum slab thickness is ¾ inches. The Mini SRC is ideal for taking to workshops or for studios with limited space. It is constructed of steel pipe and bent plate like the SRC so it will last for many years. The patented cable drive system with opposing rollers produces even pressure along the bed. It includes one ¼-in. shim with canvas and two ¼-in. plain shims. Assembled dimensions: 31W×26L×14H.

The Brent Mini SRC.

Laguna Clay Company (City of Industry, CA)
www.lagunaclay.com

The Bellar Roller Vertical Slab Roller

Designed by potter David Bellar, The Bellar Roller is manufactured and distributed through Laguna Clay Company. This vertical slab roller stands 80 inches high, 35 inches wide and only a little over 10 inches deep. The slab roller's handle can be installed for either right- or left-hand operation. The roller can be set up to operate with its free standing floor mount or against the wall. With the floor mount braces, the roller has a 30-in. deep footprint, but the wall mount option only adds $1^{5}/_{8}$ inches to the overall depth. Since it is operated vertically, Laguna's Bellar Roller takes up less studio space than many horizontally-operated rollers.

The slab thickness adjustment is labeled in both metric and inches, and both sides work in tandem. The slab roller features a flip stop mechanism next to the crank handle. It holds the canvas at full stop while the finished slab is still on the fully extended upper canvas. This allows the operator to easily use both hands while removing the slab from the unit.

The Bellar Roller, a vertical slab roller designed by David Bellar and manufactured by Laguna Clay Company. Shown with its floor mount braces.

The Bellar Roller ships boxed with wooden skids to allow use of a fork lift or safe moving by hand and weighs in at approximately 200 pounds. One canvas is included with the unit and replacement canvases are available.

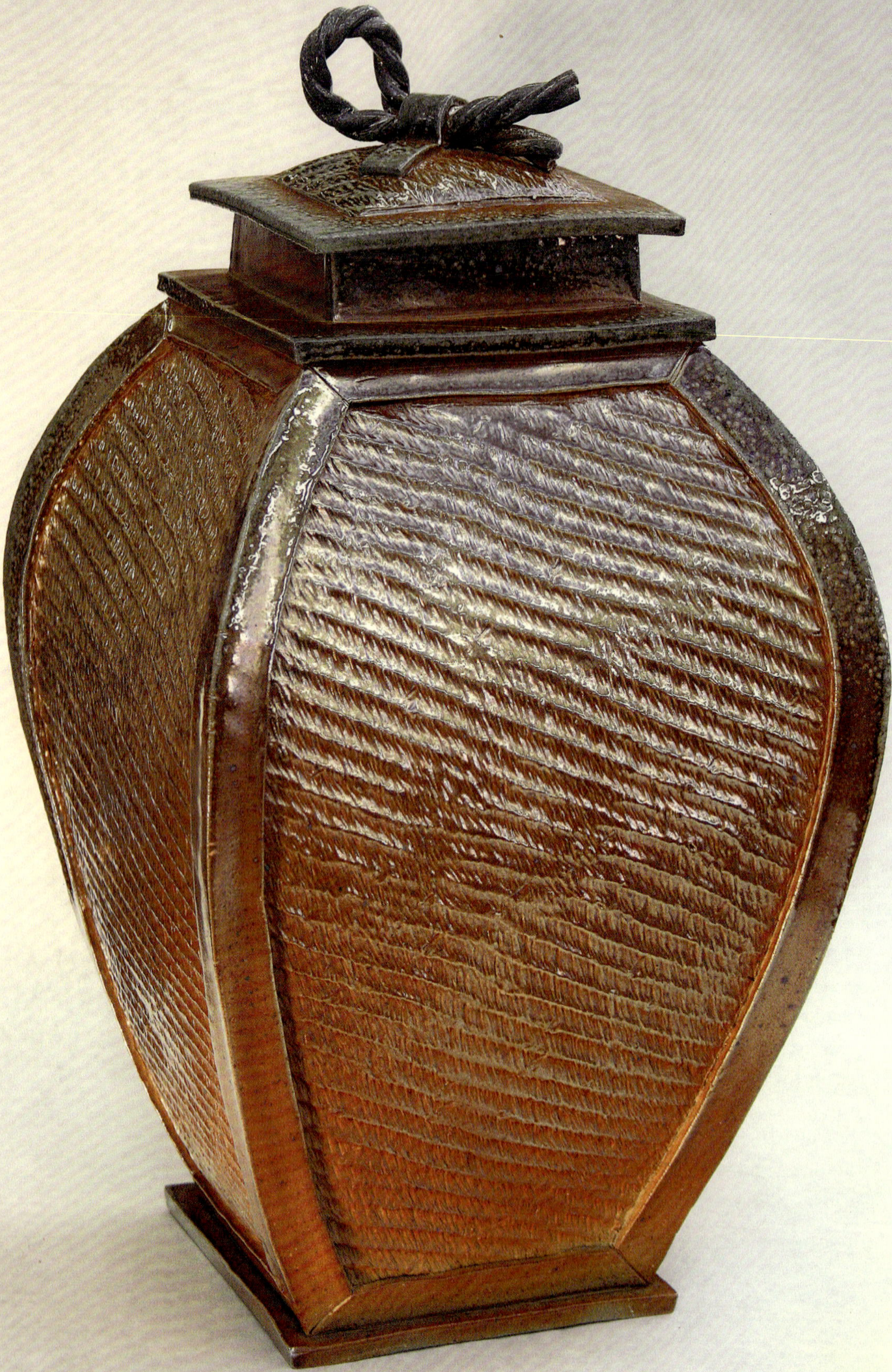

Build Your Own Slab Roller

If you do an online search for "slab roller plans," it may find a reference to George and Nancy Wettlaufer's book, *Getting Into Pots: A Basic Pottery Manual*, published in 1975. The book contains plans for building a simple slab roller and, while no longer in print, the book may be at your local library or through interlibrary loan.

George Weltlaufer's design is easy enough to build. It's simple and uses common materials, and by making a few modifications it's now even easier to make using ordinary hand tools.

All of the slab roller's parts are available at local home improvement centers so there's no need to go to a machine shop. You should be able to get everything needed in one trip; at most three.

The slab roller's base and top sheet can be cut from a full sheet of ¾-in. exterior plywood, but, in the lumber aisle there might be pre-cut pieces that suit this design very well. Most home centers will cut sheet goods for free, so be sure to ask the salesperson.

In the plumbing aisle you'll find a selection of plastic pipes in various diameters. A piece of 3-in. diameter ABS (acrylonitrile butadiene styrene) black plastic pipe is used for the roller itself. Typically this is sold in ten-foot lengths though this plan only requires a piece that is less than 30 inches long.

You'll also need some of the same pipe in a 2-in. diameter may be fortunate to find this pre-cut in a 2-ft. length. The plumbing aisle also provides most of the other parts needed for the roller assembly. The clamps needed to anchor the roller assembly to the base are in the electrical parts aisle.

Back in the lumber aisle you will want to pick up a full- or half-sheet of Masonite. It will be cut into shim boards, used to adjust the thickness of the clay as you roll it. Next, load up a bag of sand. About fifteen pounds of it is used to add ballast to the ABS pipe roller. After visiting a few more aisles, you're off to the check stand.

Jar, slab-built wood-fired stoneware,
by Fred Sweet, ht: 11 in.

MATERIALS & HARDWARE

Base & Cradle

1	¾ × 24 × 48 in. exterior plywood
10	1½ in. rubber rigid casters
20	#8 × ⅜ in. panhead screws
1	1 × 6 × 48 in. pine board
8	#8 × 1¼ in. flathead wood screws
6	#8 × 2 flathead wood screws

Guide board

1	¾ × 24 × 48 in. exterior plywood
2	¾ × 27 in. aluminum angle
10	#8 × ⅝ in. panhead screws
4	3⁄16 × 1½ in. eyebolts with nuts

Roller Assembly

1	3 in. × 27 in. ABS pipe
2	2 in. × 3½ in. ABS pipe
2	3 in. × 2 in. ABS reducing coupling
2	2 in. ABS cap
6	#8 × ⅜ in. panhead screws
4	¼ × 2½ in. round head wood screws
8	¼ in. flat washers
2	⅛ in. × 9 ft. steel cables
4	cable clamps
2	2 in. PVC conduit clamps

Hand Crank Assembly

1	⅛ × 1 × 24 in. steel bar
1	1⅜ × 5 in. dowel (from closet rod)
2	¼ - 20 × ¾ in. round head bolts
1	¼ × 2½ in. round head wood screw
4	¼ in. flat washers
2	¼ in. lock washers
2	¼ - 20 nutsTools

Construct the Base

Take one of the 2×4 foot pieces of ¾-in. plywood and mark the locations of the casters.

Attach the 10 casters with #8×⅜-in. panhead screws.

Note: All the caster axles must be perpendicular to the sides of the base to ensure the top board glides smoothly over them.

Optional: If the base is warped, you can add 2×2-in. wood rails to the underside to stabilize the plywood.

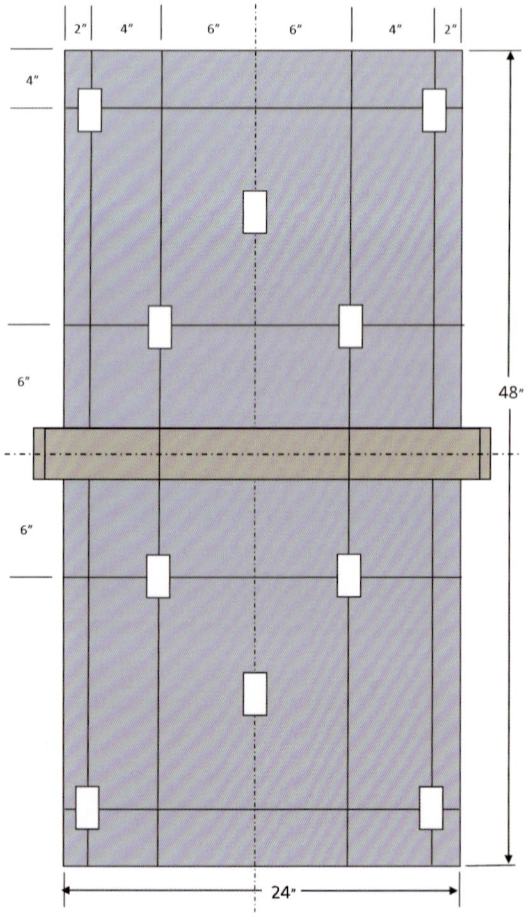

Layout of the baseboard with caster location.

Drawing not to scale

Slab-Making Options

Construct the Cradle

The roller is mounted to a cradle. To make the cradle, cut a 34-in. long section and two 5½-in. pieces from the 1×6. Cut the 5½-in. pieces down to 3 inches wide to create two 3×5½- and two 1×5½-in. pieces.

Attach the 3×5½-in. pieces to the ends of the 1×6 with three #8×2-in. flathead wood screws on each end.

Assemble roller cradle with screws.

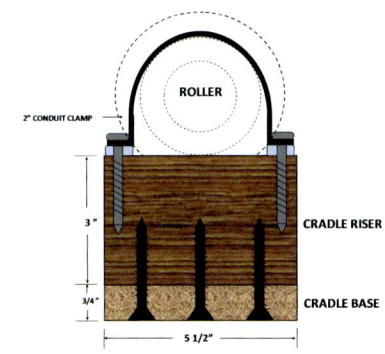

Roller cradle construction detail.

TOOLS
Indelible marker, like a Sharpie pen
Yardstick
Tape Measure
Ruler
Carpenter's Square
Screwdrivers, Philips and slotted
Hacksaw
Center Punch
Hammer
Flat File or bench grinder
Rubber Mallet
Bench Vise
Hand Drill or Drill Press with assorted drill bits
Spring Clamps (2)
Hand Saw or Table Saw
Sandpaper, 150 grit
Duct Tape
Masking Tape
Dremel-type rotary tool with bits for grinding & cutting
Open-end wrench (for tightening cable clamps)

Glue and clamp the 1-in. blocks into the inside corners to strengthen the joints.

Attach the cradle to the center of the base with eight evenly spaced #8×1¼-in. flathead wood screws. Hold the cradle in place with clamps as you drill pilot holes and attach with screws.

Remove the clamps. At this point, I added two rails to the bottom of the base board to correct a slight warp. I extended the rails past the ends of the slab roller to make it easier to pick up and transport. The rails are not essential if the base board is flat.

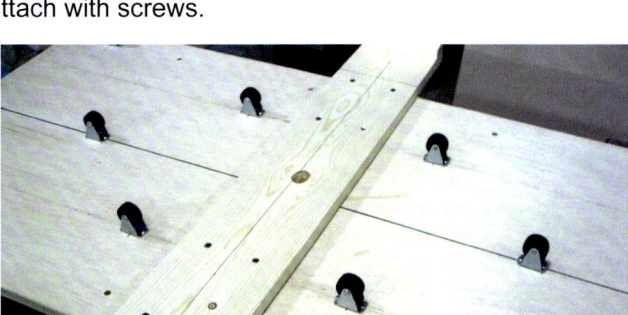

Attach the cradle to the baseboard with screws.

From a Slab of Clay

Make the Glide Board

Cut two 27-in. lengths of ¾-in. aluminum angle. Use a flat file or grinder to remove any burrs.

Draw a line at the mid-point of each angle piece and drill 11/64-in. holes in each piece for the screws and two 3/16-in. holes for the eyebolts.

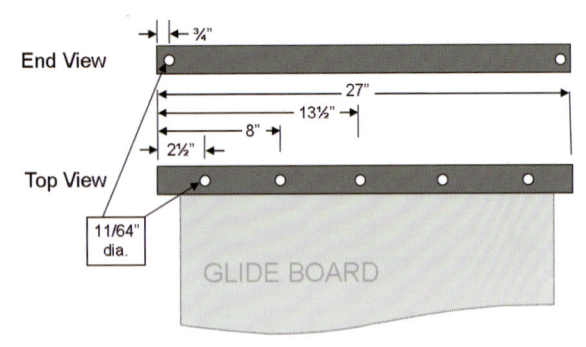

Attach the angle aluminum to each end of the 2×4-ft. plywood glide board using #8×5/8-in. panhead screws.

Loosely attach the eye bolts to each end of the aluminum angles with the eye of each bolt pointing inward. At this point, the base board and glide board subassemblies are finished.

Drilling plan for aluminum angle.

Build the Roller

Cut one 27-in. long piece of 3-in. diameter ABS pipe, and two 3½-in. long pieces of 2-in. diameter ABS pipe. Sand rough edges. Note: All cuts must be 90° so using a miter box or miter saw is recommended.

Prepare the reducers by removing any raised mold ridges with a Dremel-type tool or small grinder to create a smooth surface. Use a rubber mallet to tap the reducers onto each end of the 3-in. pipe.

Tap a 2-in. diameter ABS piece into the reducer on one end only. (The other end goes on after the crank is made.) Fully seat the pieces. Note: PVC pipe adhesive is not used in this assembly.

ABS plastic part for roller assembly.

Tap a cap onto one end of the roller.

Slab-Making Options

Make & Assemble the Crank

Mark the center line of the other 2-in. ABS cap and drill a ¼-in. hole ¾ inches on either side of this line.

Use a hacksaw to cut a 24-in. long piece of flat iron bar. Measure in an inch from one end of the handle and drill a ¼-in.-diameter hole using a metal cutting drill bit. For the mounting holes, drill two ¼-in. holes one on the other end using the ABS end cap from the previous step as a guide for drilling the holes.

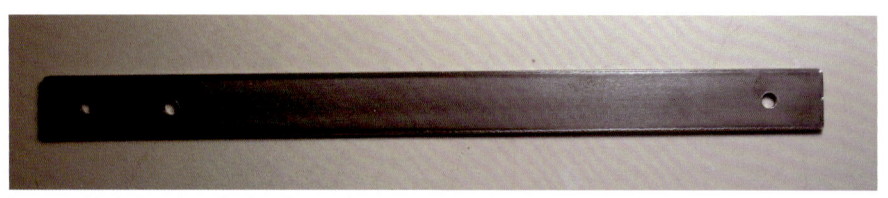

Layout of hole locations for handle crank.

Attach the end cap to the bar using two ¼-20×¾-in. machine screws. Use flat washers on the outside of the cap and lock washers on the inside. Note: It's important that these attachments stay tight for the life of the roller. As an added precaution, apply Loctite threadlock adhesive before tightening.

Crank and end cap detail.

Make the wooden handle from a 5-in. long piece of closet pole. Drill a pilot hole through the center on one end and attach the handle to the crank with a ¼×2½-in. roundhead wood screw and a flat washer on each side of the crank. Tighten the screw all the way down then loosen it just enough to allow the grip to turn smoothly.

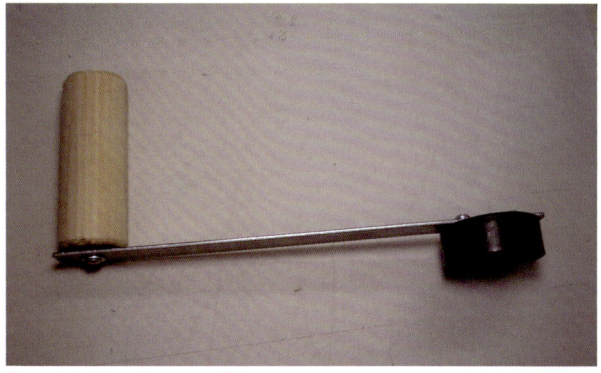

Completed handle assembly.

From a Slab of Clay

Assemble the Roller

Fill the roller with playground sand, plaster, or concrete. When using sand, tap the pipe to compact the sand. No matter what material you use, have someone hold the pipe while you fill it.

When the roller is completely filled, tap the crank onto the open end.

Attach the Roller

Lay the roller onto the cradle and place a U-shaped 2-in. conduit clamp over each of roller end. While holding an anchor in place, drill two pilot holes in the cradle. Repeat for the other end of the cradle.

To help the roller turn freely under the anchors, place two flat washers under each of the mounting holes to act as shims. Secure the conduit anchors using #10×2½-in. roundhead wood screws with a flat washer under the head of each. The roller should turn smoothly under the anchors without extra effort. Do not overtighten the screws.

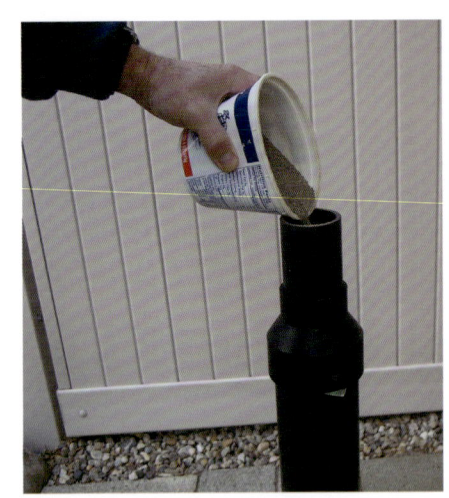

Fill the roller with sand for ballast.

Mounting detail for roller end.

Install the glide board on top of the casters then turn the hand crank and check the gap between the glide board and the bottom of the roller in several locations. The gap should be the same at each stopping point across the full length of the roller. If it isn't, the thickness of the slab will vary. Remove the roller assembly, if necessary, and use the mallet to square up the reducer and other roller components. Reinstall the roller assembly and check the uniformity of the gap. When the gap is right, continue with the installation of the cables.

Slab-Making Options

Attach the Cables

Fold the 9-ft. cables in half to find the midpoint, being careful not to crimp them, and mark this point with an indelible marker.

Lay a cable across the open jaws of a bench vise and, using a hammer, drive a small nail through the strands of the cable. Take care to get an even number of strands on either side of the nail. Before removing the small nail, tap a larger nail into the opening and remove the small nail. Work the large nail back and forth to widen the opening in the cable.

Before you remove the large nail, insert a #8×3/8-in. screw into the opening then remove the nail. Leave the screw in place. Repeat this for the other cable.

Turn the roller so the handle is pointing straight down then drill a 1/8-in. pilot hole in the center of the large end of the reducer. Attach a cable with a #8×3/8-in. screw into place. Repeat this for the other cable.

If it isn't already in place on top of the casters, slide the glide board under the roller to the right, leaving about 2 inches of the board exposed on the left of the roller. Stand at the crank side of the roller and slide the left end of the cable under the roller to the right. Thread this end of the

Mark the center of each cable.

Insert nail into cable to separate wires.

Insert screw into cable.

Cable to aluminum angle assembly detail.

45

From a Slab of Clay

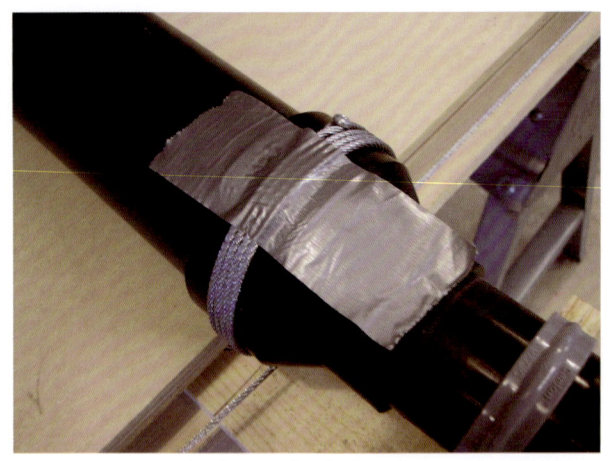

Another use for duct tape!

cable through the eye bolt then loop it over onto itself and hold it in place, loosely, with a cable clamp. Move around to the other side of the roller and attach the other cable to the same end of the glide board.

Tip: Before attaching the other ends of the cables, have two 5-in. lengths of duct tape at the ready. When each cable is wound around the roller, use the duct tape to hold the windings in place while attaching the cable to the eye bolt.

Move back to the crank side of the roller and wrap the right end of the cable around the roller three times and have it come out under the roller to the left. Thread this end of the cable through the eye bolt, loop it onto itself and secure, loosely, with a cable clamp. Repeat this for the other cable. All four ends of the cables should now be attached to the eye bolts in the glide board.

Adjust the Cables

At this point the cables are very loose and likely to slide off the roller if the hand crank is turned. Carefully turn the crank so the middle of the glide board is under the roller. Take care to keep the cable wraps from unwinding. Reapply the duct tape if necessary.

Turn the nut on each eye bolt so only a few threads are showing past the end of the nut. This allows for maximum adjustment travel.

Loosen a cable clamp so the slack can be pulled out of one side of a cable. Keep the edges of the glide board squared up with the edges of the base board during all of the adjustments. As the slack is drawn out, tighten the clamp using a wrench. Repeat this for the other three cable ends. At this stage, most of the slack is out of the cables but fine adjustment may still be necessary.

Turn the hand crank and observe the movement of the glide board. Use a wrench to turn the nuts on the eyebolts and tighten the cables. If the glide board drifts to one side, try tightening the cable on the other side. By trial, the tension in the cables will reach the point where the cable windings on the roller stay flat and the glide board remains square as it moves under the roller.

Leave two inches of cable past the end of the clamp and cut off the excess. Cable cutters are ideal for this but a Dremel-type tool equipped with a cutting disk serves the purpose as well. Tape the end of the cable to prevent snagging.

Using the Slab Roller

Make two shim boards from a sheet of 3/16-in. tempered hardboard (Masonite). As designed, this slab roller has a 3/4-in. gap between the bottom of the roller and the top of the glide board. This is a light-duty slab roller so a thin slab of clay is developed by rolling the clay several times and adding shim boards with each pass to narrow the gap. Rolling a large, stiff mass of clay with both shim boards in place at once is likely to damage the roller.

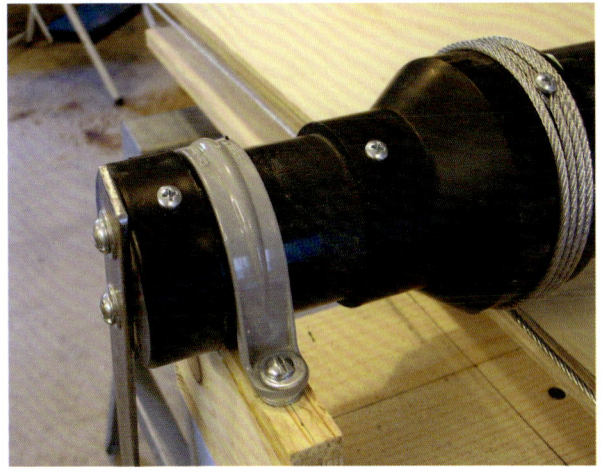

Set screw detail on crank end of roller.

For the first pass, place the clay directly on the glide board. Since clay will stick to the ABS roller, cover the clay with a piece of canvas or bed sheet. When satisfied that the slab roller is operating satisfactorily, install #8×3/8-in. screws in the narrow ends of the reducers and in the end caps. The set screws will help keep the roller components in place.

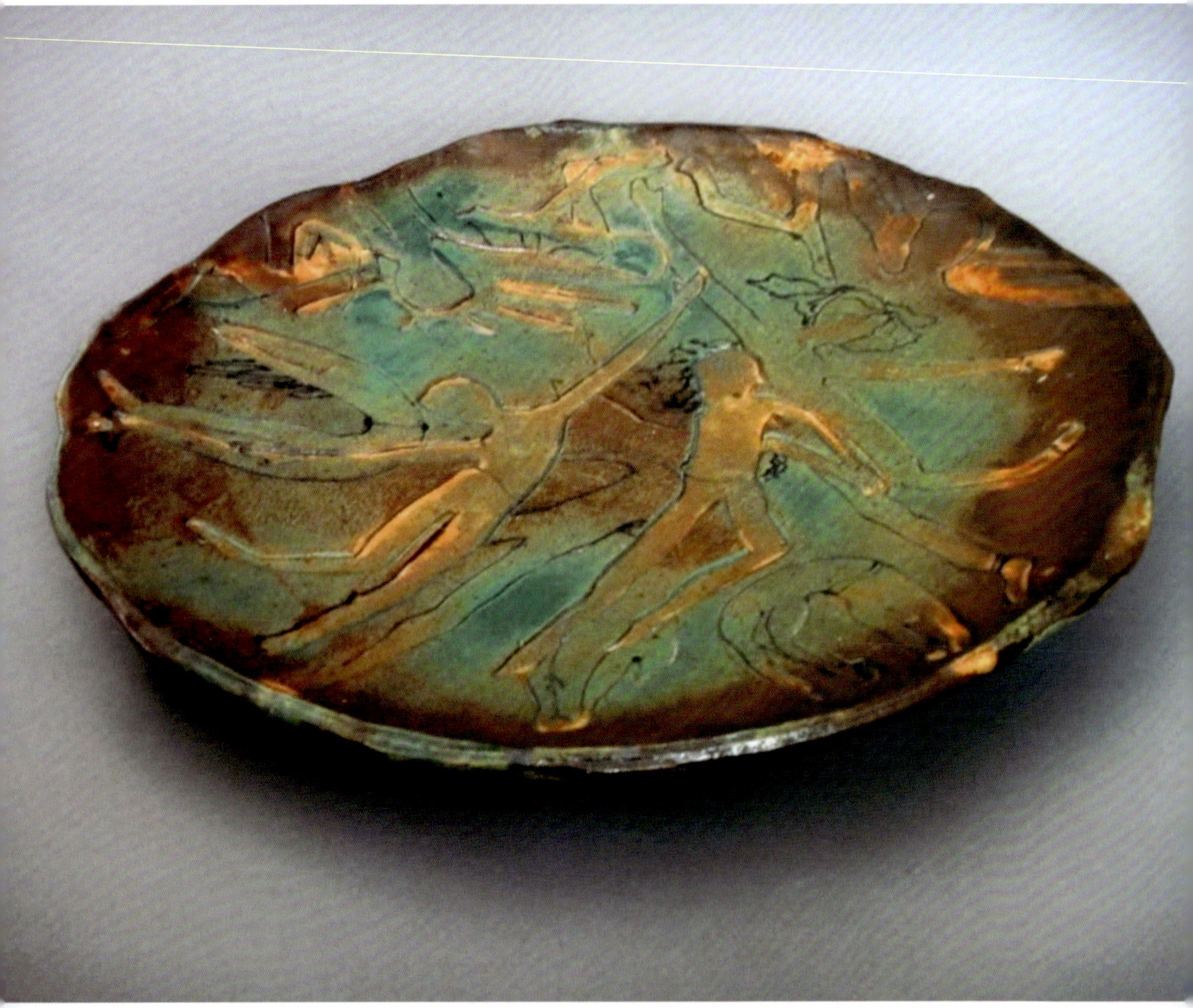

CHAPTER **4**

Tools

If just starting out with clay, you may think you don't have a lot of clay tools. In reality, you have a many clay tools and they are no farther away than your kitchen or garage.

Having dozens of clay tools is by no means a prerequisite for slab work. But, don't be surprised as you work on your initial projects that you start looking at the utensils in your kitchen drawers or at the hand tools in your garage and find yourself thinking, "I wonder how those would work on clay?" If so, good for you!

You've gone through the house and garage and taken everything there. Where next? Second-hand stores, hardware stores, home improvement centers and, of course, the place where you bought your clay are all prime hunting grounds for slab tools.

But wait, there's still another source: the good old trash. No one is suggesting that you rummage through your own garbage. No, but the trash at building sites can yield some choice finds. One of the first workshops I attended was conducted by noted clay artist, Robert Piepenburg. Among the many techniques demonstrated, Robert pressed the edges of scrap wooden molding into his clay to create very distinctive effects. One small piece of molding offered a variety of interesting marks just by altering how it was pressed into the clay. His techniques were done on wheel-thrown clay, but they apply perfectly to slab work.

Smoothers

For many projects, you'll want to give the slab a smooth surface and there is a wide array of tools suited for this.

Painting edge tools. These are available at most hardware and home improvement centers that offer painting supplies, and are 24 inches wide and have a rigid metal blade. When gripped with two hands, the painting edge tool can be pulled across the surface of the clay to easily remove most surface imperfections.

Dancing Charger, stoneware impressed with cut-out shapes, wheel-thrown foot, black slip trailed on barium carbonate matte glaze applied with iron overspray, fired to cone 10, by Karmien Bowman.

Putty knives. These come in a variety of widths, from 2 to 8 inches. Putty knives are available with either stainless steel or plastic blades. The stainless steel models will retain a smooth edge almost indefinitely while the less expensive plastic variety will show some wear over time, especially when used over coarse clays. Putty knives are suited for smoothing smaller slabs of clay and for getting into the tight spaces of assembled projects.

It's easy to assemble a nice collection of edged tools for scraping and smoothing slabs. Clockwise from the left, long edge tools used for painting trim and cutting wallpaper, a simple block of wood, molding, ruler, ribs (metal, wood and plastic, credit cards and putty knives.

Rulers. The ordinary wooden ruler is another of the slab maker's essentials. It's easy to manage by even the smallest hands and does an excellent job of smoothing slabs that are less than 12 inches wide.

Rollers. These were covered extensively in Chapter 3, but the list of smoothers is incomplete without rollers like the pony roller shown here. As you saw, rollers, large and small, are also members of the texture-maker toolset.

A selection of rollers for smoothing clay. Left to right, a rubber-covered printing brayer, a pony roller, an inexpensive carpet or wallpaper seam roller and two rollers from produce department tear-off bags.

Yardsticks. While the painting edge tool, described above, is ideal for smoothing the surface of large slabs, a yardstick can do a very good job provided at least one of its four edges is free of damage. One important consideration: Many of the inexpensive wooden yardsticks sold in the paint departments of hardware stores are made of soft wood that is vulnerable dings and dents. Metal yardsticks sold in tool departments, while many times more expensive than the wooden variety, offer many more years of service and much better results.

Potter's ribs. As the name indicates, these are used by potters who are smoothing the flat and contoured surfaces of wheel-thrown pottery. Here, too, there are many types available and virtually all of them are of some use in making things from slabs. Most pottery supply companies carry a full complement of potter's ribs from which to select.

Found objects. As you've guessed, these smoothers are items that had a life as something else and have new life in your tool collection. The back of a hacksaw blade, a piece of tile, a slat from a window blind, a length of metal strapping — all become excellent smoothers.

Texture-makers

This is where the fun of collecting clay tools really begins. It would almost be easier to list the things that don't make good tools for texturing your clay than to list all of those that do. But, let's give it a shot, at least on a macro level.

Plastic mesh bags (potato or onion)	Old combs and hair rollers	Tree bark and leaves
Egg cartons (use the lids as slump/drape molds)	Costume jewelry	Seashells
	Shoe treads	Driftwood
Aluminum foil (wad up then open up and flatten it for texture)	Fabric scraps	Plaster casts of animal prints
	Throw rug backing	Weathered boards
	Tire treads	Stepping stones
Pastas and cereals	Floor mats	Decking
Forks, graters, spatulas, potato maskers	Hand rake (makes wavy lines)	Concrete
	Hand weeder (makes fish scales)	

Years ago I watched Montana clay artist and instructor David Scott Smith painstakingly cast a mold from a real snake then another from a bat. What impressed me most was the textural detail that was revealed in the plaster. Our eyes are more conditioned to focus on colors and when they are removed, we can detect the texture more readily. You might very well have the same experience as you press things into clay. Each object's texture will become much more obvious to you.

Texture hunts often occur spontaneously, without a lot of forethought. You may be caught without the materials you need for capturing textures. No matter, just note the location and plan your return. Before heading back you might assemble sort of a "field studio." Make several slabs of clay and wrap them in plastic. Take a couple of slab boards, a rolling pin and something you can use to cut the clay. Take everything you need to mix a small batch of pottery plaster: a plastic bucket, stir stick, pre-measured water and pre-measured plaster.

Rolling Pins

The rolling pin is ideal for modifying so they can be used to impart textures to clay. A variety of materials can be attached to a rolling pin so that it will create imprints in clay. Making your own rollers and experimenting with the textures they make can really be a lot of fun. The key is to experiment and to keep working with a roller even if the desired results are not immediately obtained.

Wood veneer. This is thin and flexible. Several pieces can be cut out with a scroll saw then soaked in water to soften. Wrapped around a roller while damp, the pieces will dry and can be glued into place.

Cork sheets. We found this at an auto supply shop. It's used for making gaskets. It's easily cut with an X-Acto knife (#11 blade) and can be glued onto a cardboard tube or rolling pin with contact cement.

Nails, tacks or screws. Designs can be made with a mix of shapes and they can be combined with other materials for even more variety.

Textured wallpaper. This can be glued over a length of plastic drain pipe for an inexpensive texture-maker.

Embossed ceiling tile. The antique copper variety may be too precious for this, but reproductions made from vinyl are supplied by Ceilume (Windsor, CA).

Linoleum floor tile. This is also used for linocut printmaking. This material hardens over time so use fresh, soft tiles. A 12×12-in. tile can be cut down to wrap completely around a 3-in. cylinder. To make more flexible, warm it with a hair dryer or heat gun.

Glues and latex caulk. Choose an adhesive that offers a comfortable amount of working time before it hardens. Once cured, it can be trimmed with a razor blade or utility knife. You can create an endless variety of stamps, paddles and patterns by applying hot glue dots and lines to tools. The results achieved with cardboard cylinders are particularly nice; these can be slipped over a rolling pin and used to pattern slabs.

> Clay may stick to some of the "texture makers" you try. This may not pose a problem if the roller is worked quickly over the surface. Even if the clay does stick, it may bring about some desirable results. Still, to cure the "stickies," apply a light dusting of talcum powder or corn starch to the roller.

Rope, cord or string. Any sturdy cylinder tightly wrapped with rope, cord or string makes a roller that will impart interesting texture to clay. Epoxy or any other strong adhesive should be used to bond the cord to the roller.

Roulettes and Stamps

Roulettes, or small texture rollers, and stamps present a wonderful creative outlet. They are easy to design and simple to make from ordinary materials you probably already have, and there's a large selection of ready-made roulettes and texture rollers available from suppliers. Here's just a short list of materials that can be used for making your own roulettes and stamps: plaster, pottery clay and self-hardening clay, polymer clay (like Sculpey or Fimo brands), bottle corks, chalk, insulation board and any of the soft woods. Some ink stamps make nice imprints in clay but these often prove to be too "mushy" or over-detailed for all but the softest, finest clays. Some shops and online businesses can make custom stamps cast in resin for you. These are much harder and make deeper, better defined imprints. Tip: When ordering a custom made stamp, be sure to stipulate how you want the stamp to "read" when you use it—as is or a mirror image.

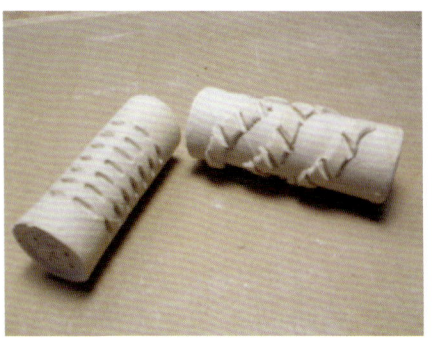

Two roulettes made from clay. Clay roulettes can be fired or used when just bone dry.

This short plaster roulette works for decorative borders. A hole was drilled for a small dowel.

You can purchase roulettes and texture rollers in a wide variety of designs like this texture roller from Amaco. Photo courtesy David Gamble.

Make Your Own Roulettes and Stamps

Texture rollers made by cutting shapes from a sheet of cork and gluing them to sturdy cardboard tubes with contact cement.

Puffy Paint from the fabric department adheres nicely to cardboard tubes and is ready for rolling the next day.

Polymer clays such as Sculpey and FIMO make great stamps that are ready to use in 30 minutes. Play-Doh also works but takes a while to harden.

Draw the design on the cork with a pen then use a knife or rotary tool to cut it out. Mistakes can be sanded off.

How to Make Rolling Stamps

Roll out a ³/₈-in. thick slab and create designs by carving, stamping or adding sprigs. Cut the clay into strips.

Allow the slab to set up on a curved surface then add a handle when leather hard. Cut a hole in the center of each handle to make it easier to grip.

Test each of the stamps on fresh clay before firing to see if refinements to the design are necessary.

Rolling stamps made from clay slabs. After bisque firing, these stamps can be used for years.

How to Make Plaster Roulettes

Cut paper tubes into 6-in. lengths. Set them in a shallow pan and hold them in place with a soft clay coil. The coil also holds the plaster in.

Mix plaster and spoon into each cylinder. After filling, pick up the plate and lightly tap it on the table to help release any air bubbles.

Allow the plaster to set up, then while the tube is moist, peel it off. Remove cardboard remnants with a sponge and water.

Saw off the rough end of each plaster blank, and sand smooth. Carve the blanks and test. Allow the plaster to thoroughly dry before using.

Creating and Using Stencils

Karmien Bowman of Flower Mound, TX, creates stencils from pieces of thin cardboard. She places shapes on a slab then brushes on slip.

After the slip sets up, she carefully removes the shapes. This needs to be done before the slip dries, otherwise it cracks off.

Here Karmien uses a metal ring to locate the best image and then cuts through the slab. Any shape can be cut using a fettling knife.

Finished shapes that have been allowed to set up over drape molds. Colored slips add distinctive designs to rolled slabs.

Creating Shape Plates

Karmien also creates "shape plates" using patterns cut from thick cardboard or tempered hardboard. She arranges the template on the clay.

After rolling the pattern into the clay, she carefully pries it out using a needle tool to reveal a recessed design.

The slab is cut to its final shape and allowed to set up. It can either dry flat or be placed on a drape mold or in a slump mold.

Colored slips can be added to highlight the recessed pattern.

Cutters

Now to the practical matter of cutting the clay slabs down to size. There really isn't a need to assemble a large collection of tools. A few select cutters will serve your needs completely. Your clay supplier offers metal ribs in many sizes and shapes. The rigid varieties make good cutters. Your supplier also has a nice selection of clay knives. Look for those that are fashioned from hardwoods or bamboo. They are shaped to fit comfortably in your hand; they keep their edge and can last a lifetime.

You can also make clay cutters from Popsicle sticks or tongue depressors. These glide through most clay easily. For heavier work, a wooden paint stirring stick can be shaped into a suitable cutter. All of these are made from soft wood and won't hold an edge under heavy use.

Putty knives and the painting edge tool do an excellent job of cutting, especially on very firm slabs. Their blades can be pushed down and through slabs for clean, straight cuts.

Finally, a pizza cutter, the type with a handle and a rolling blade, is safe and easy to handle. The blade is very narrow so it cuts through the clay very cleanly. A pizza cutter is especially useful when cutting square or rectangular tile.

A nice assortment of cutters ranging from a paint edge trimmer and serrated edge knife to various wooden tools and ribs.

More cutters (l to r): a small rolling cutter, a pizza cutter and two putty knives.

Joiners

Joiners are simply the tools you use to prepare clay so that pieces can be attached. The bond has to be strong to avoid cracking. A tool that can efficiently rough up or "score" the edges of the clay is essential. Your clay supplier offers serrated ribs in two or three sizes. Each comes in very handy for scoring your clay edges and getting them ready for coating with clay slip and attaching the pieces. We'll cover scoring and slipping in more detail in the Demonstrations chapter. Also considered tools for joining are small brushes and toothbrushes, which help spread the slip before assembly.

This category includes tools you use to finish the seams after joining the edges. A wedge-shaped pencil eraser fitted onto the handle of a needle tool works well for joining slabs or thrown sections. The rubber is soft and pliant like a small fingertip, but able to reach into tight places. Manufactured rubber tipped tools are also available. Disposable wooden chopsticks are very useful when cleaning up interior seams on slab-built boxes. They have a long reach and their square edge finishes off the seam cleanly. For the outside corner of boxes, a tool used to remove excess tub and shower caulk is good and available at any home center.

Joiners (l to r): a wooden block for smoothing angular joints, rubber-tipped clean-up tools, a toothbrush, needle tool, large serrated rib, serrated half-ribs and a serrated rib like that from which the half-ribs were made.

Profilers

Among the select tools used to give projects a finished appearance are those regarded as "profiles" or "edgers." Potters traditionally use these to give a finished edge to the bottom and rim of a wheel-thrown vessel. But, they work very well in rounding off the square-cut edge of slabs. A profile tool drawn around the rim of a cup or tankard made from a rolled slab will help make it feel lip-friendly.

Profile tools can be made from hardwood or metal. In a pinch, a profile can even be made from an old credit card or scrap plastic. A jeweler's saw or scroll saw can be used to cut out the basic shape. Then, a Dremel-type rotary tool and several bits, including those for grinding, sanding and polishing, can be used to give the profile a nice finish.

Profiles or edgers are available as hardwood sticks with profile tips, or you can modify a wooden rib. The Ultimate Edger is made from stainless steel and is offered in two sizes. It is available from most pottery tool suppliers.

Measuring Aids

It's important to have several measurement tools close at hand when working with your clay slabs. These include:

Yardsticks and rulers. These are listed among our smoothers but you'll need them for routine measurements as well.

Carpenter's squares. Also called framing squares, these have a 24-in. blade and a 16-in. tongue, forming a right (90°) angle. The blade and tongue are marked with inches and fractions of an inch, or their metric equivalents. The blade and the tongue can also be used as a rule or a straightedge. Tables and formulas are printed on the blade for making quick calculations such as determining area and volume. Very handy.

Picture frame. If its edges are free of dings and cracks and if sturdy, you have the makings for a do-it-yourself carpenter's square. You can leave all four of the sides intact or saw it down to make two squares. You can customize your "picture frame square" by adding any measurement marks you want.

Protractor. If you're planning projects with geometrical elements, a protractor will prove useful. It's easy to lay out any angle with it.

French curve. This is a template made from plastic, metal or wood. It is composed of many different curves. It is commonly used in manual drafting to draw smooth curves of varying radii and it can be used on clay the same way. The selected curve is placed on the slab and a needle tool or knife is traced around its curves to produce the desired result. French curves can be found where drafting supplies are sold.

Cloth tape measure. This is useful for quickly measuring an object's circumference – without having to do any math!

> If you want to wrap a slab of clay around a cylindrical form, you can easily determine how long your slab needs to be so that it will make it all the way around the form. Measure the form's diameter then multiply that by 3.14. Add a fraction of an inch for overlap and you're ready to roll!

A sturdy, wooden picture frame makes a good cutting guide.

THE CLAY RULER

If you want something you're making to be a specific size when finished, you have to compensate for the clay's shrinkage. For example, if you wanted to make a ceramic cover for a tissue box you would take the height, width and depth measurements from the tissue box then, when cutting out the slabs, you would increase each dimension to allow for shrinkage. But, how much? A ruler made from clay, can help you determine how much larger you need to cut your slabs so that your finished project has the desired dimensions. Here's how to do it:

1. Roll out a ⅜-in. thick slab and cut a 3×16 inch rectangle from the center of it.

2. Allow the rectangle to firm up to about the consistency of the slabs you plan to cut up for your project.

3. Lay a ruler or yardstick next to the rectangular slab and carefully transfer the increments from the ruler to the clay. Hand number or use stamps to label each of the one-inch increments. Or press a ruler that has raised numbers and marks into the clay slab. The numbers in the imprint will be backwards but the clay ruler will still be easy to read.

4. Take precautions to ensure that the clay ruler dries flat then fire it to the clay's maturity temperature.

5. Use the clay ruler to measure the tissue box, and read each measurement from the clay ruler.

A fired clay ruler can tell you how big you need to make a piece to allow for shrinkage. The inch marks are closer together because the ruler shrank, but this measurment tells you how big the original should be.

In the example of the tissue box, the clay ruler says the width and depth are 5 inches and the height is 6 inches. Add ¼ inch to each measurement so the cover doesn't fit over the tissue box too snugly. These are the measurements used to make the tissue box cover. Bear in mind that these are the dimensions for the interior of the box cover. Using these measurements and a wooden ruler, yardstick or carpenter's square, the pieces for the sides and top of the tissue box cover can be cut out.

The Other Stuff

While not tools, in the literal sense, there are a few items that are so useful in slab making that they warrant inclusion here.

Dry cleaning bags. This soft, yet sturdy, plastic sheeting is a great boon for keeping clay soft and workable. In their book, *Slab Techniques,* Jim Robison and Ian Marsh suggest placing paper or cloth over slabs or work in progress prior to wrapping them in plastic. If there is any air space around the clay, moisture from the clay evaporates and condenses on the plastic. The clay continues to dry out and water droplets often run down the plastic, sometimes streaking the work in progress. Paper or cloth collects this water, keeping it next to the slabs and helping to maintain a uniform softness in the clay.

Dry cleaning bags are also useful for long-term slab storage. Several clay slabs can be made in advance then layered between plastic sheets and stored in a Styrofoam cooler. The bags make it easy to lift the slabs from the cooler.

Dry cleaning bags are useful in decorating. Place a piece over any surface to be patterned with fine-line incising, then simply use a pencil to impress the design. The resulting lines will be burr-free.

Cardboard tubes. Collect the sturdiest you can find in a variety of diameters and lengths. To use cardboard cylinders as forms for slab projects such as vases, jars or mugs, try wrapping the cardboard with aluminum foil.

Elastic bandages. These are used to wrap a sprained ankle but they offer excellent support for slab-built sculptures. The elastic stretches to fit almost any shape or size then shrinks with the work as it dries

Storage

Most of the tools listed can be stored in a 36x60 inch cabinet. Yet, it's plain to see that if you assemble a large collection of stamps and other texture-makers you will quickly outgrow your this. Transparent, stackable food storage containers are ideal for storing and retrieving the small things. A couple of 32-gallon trash cans and their lids will prove very useful. One can hold all of the plastic bags you will use and the other will hold your rags and towels.

If you find you enjoy making and using several rolling pins and other rollers for texturing your clay slabs, consider building a rack to store and display them. At the very least these should be stored in a tub or sturdy box where they won't be at risk of damage.

> If clay sticks to the roller when rolling out slabs, try using a piece of ordinary plastic on top of the clay. In addition to keeping your roller clean and the clay free of unwanted texture, the plastic also allows you to see through and check the progress of the slab as you work.

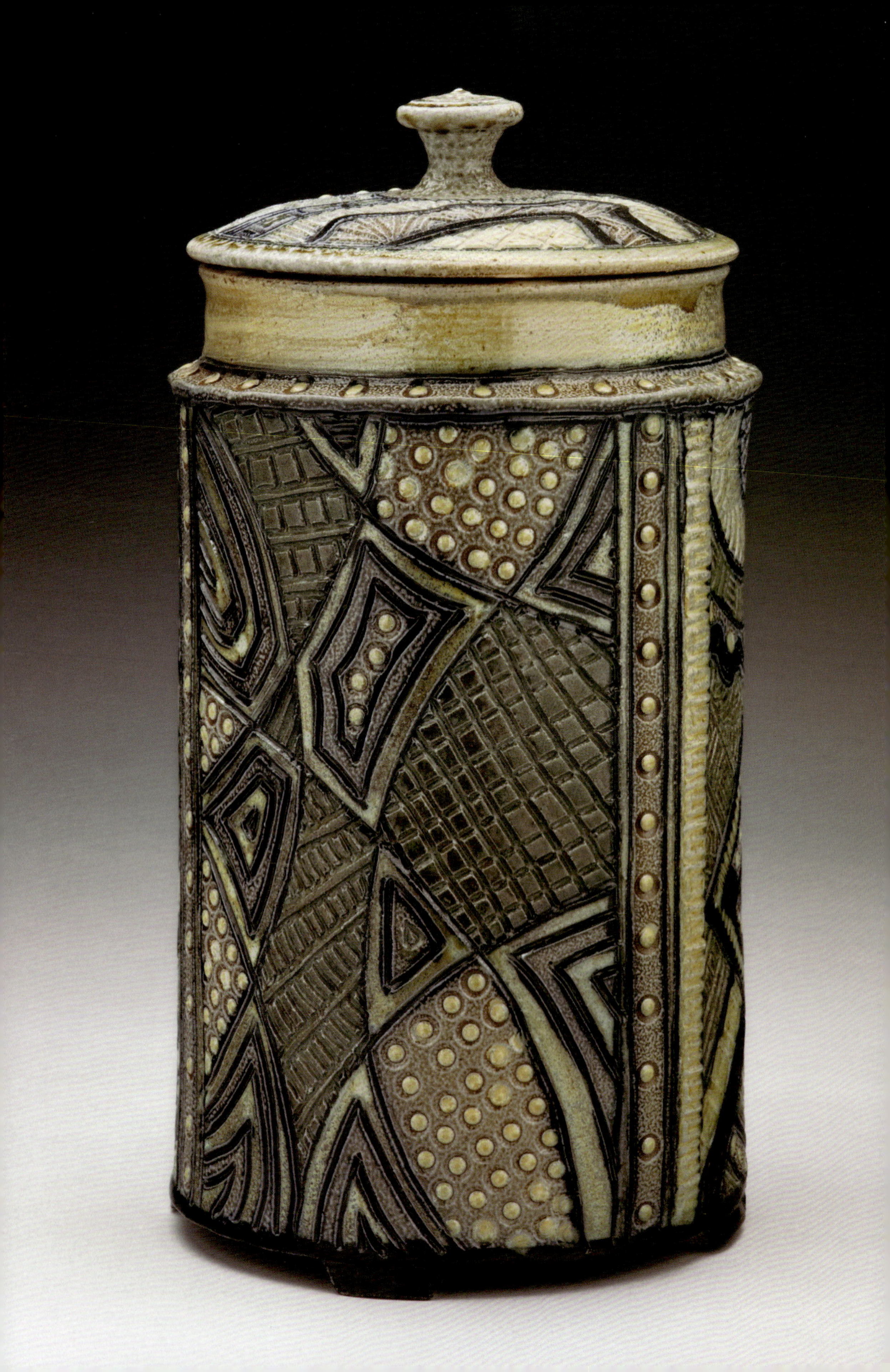

CHAPTER **5**

Demonstrations

There it is, in front of you—a freshly rolled slab of clay. It's about $3/8$ inch thick and 15 inches in diameter. In this pristine state it's almost like a blank canvas. And in the same way a novice painter may find the blank canvas a little intimidating, you may find yourself looking at the slab of clay and wondering where to start, wondering what to do with it.

Simple as it may seem, tile making is the perfect way to begin working with slabs of clay. It helps familiarize you with your clay and with the essential tools used in most slab work including: slab boards, a rolling pin or slab roller, measuring, cutting and decorating tools.

So, that's where our demonstrations start—with three different ways a square of soft clay can be turned into a tile. Each of the subsequent demonstrations is designed to build off of the tilemaking basics and to present new techniques or different ways to apply familiar techniques. Several tools are also demonstrated—some utilitarian and a few, like the miter press and the half-rib, that were designed to accomplish very specific slab-building tasks.

Before getting started, make a few prototypes where you can master the techniques and discover the textures that will increase the likelihood your projects will come out of the kiln just the way you want.

Jar, slab-built with thrown lid and lid seat. Textured with texture mat, slip decoration, salt fired to cone 10, by Ginger Steele.

From a Slab of Clay

Demonstration 1: Making a Three Tile Panel

TOOLS & MATERIALS
Needle tool, metal rib, pizza cutter, carpenter's square, slab board

A well-rolled slab of clay is the starting point for any slab project and being able to cut straight-edge shapes from it is one of the first techniques to master. Here is a demonstration on how to make a long slab and cut it to create a 3-tile panel.

1. Roll out a slab then inscribe a design into it using a stick with a rounded tip.

2. Use a needle tool or fettling knife along a carpenter's square to cut from the center-most area of the slab and from the outside edge to the center so the corners stay square.

3. A sturdy picture frame can also be used for cutting tiles. Marks on the frame make it easy to cut tiles the same size without re-measuring.

4. Finished tiles ready for controlled drying. Because the design was made before the tiles were cut out, the edges of the tiles remain intact.

66

Demonstrations

Demonstration 2: Carving a Foam Press Mold

TOOLS & MATERIALS

Charcoal stick, a soft lead pencil with eraser, paper, indelible marker, a block of foam insulation, Dremel-type rotary tool, X-Acto knife with No. 11 blade, small roller, straightedge, needle tool or cutting knife.

Slabs of fresh soft clay are perfect for pressing designs into. Here's an easy-to-make foam mold with limitless design and texture possibilities.

1. Draw or use the computer to create a design and print it in black and white. Carefully define the details with a charcoal stick or pencil.

2. Lay a block of rigid foam on top of the design. Align the block carefully to avoid smearing the design.

3. Flip the foam block with the paper design over and transfer the design to the block by rubbing a pencil eraser over it.

4. Lift the design to check the progress. If more areas need to be rubbed, carefully replace the design and continue rubbing.

From a Slab of Clay

5. Use a black marker to darken the areas of the design that will not be carved.

6. Use a rotary tool to cut away the light areas of the design. You'll need to experiment with several tips to find the one that works best.

7. Clean up the corners of the design with an X-Acto knife fitted with a fresh No. 11 blade.

8. Trim a slab of soft clay slab so that it extends an inch beyond all sides of the mold. Apply even pressure over the over with a small rolling pin.

9. Flip the clay and press mold over onto paper or fabric. Use a small roller to press the clay more deeply into the mold.

10. Flip the tile over and gently rock it while lifting. Inspect the tile to see where improvements need to be made. Cut away any undercuts and deepen shallow areas as needed.

Demonstration 3: Using a Plaster Press Mold

TOOLS & MATERIALS
Pony roller, small block of wood, rubber mallet and rubber-tipped cleaning tool

A quick way to make multiples of a tile is to first create a model of the tile then make a plaster mold of it. Here's how to use the mold once it's set up and dry.

1. Prepare a clean, dry plaster mold for pressing a tile by scraping away some rough areas in its design. Make sure all plaster chips and dust are cleared off the mold before you begin.

2. Roll out a slab of soft clay. Measure the length, width and depth of the opening and make the slab slightly longer, wider and thicker. Place the slab on the mold.

3. Roll the clay evenly into the mold, starting at the center and working outward in all directions.

4. After rolling, press the clay into the mold at the edges by hand.

From a Slab of Clay

5. Optionally, use a rubber mallet and a small block of wood to compress the clay even more.

6. Scrape away excess clay at the edges with your fingers then roll the clay from the center, outward, in all directions. Scrape excess away until the clay is flush with the mold.

7. Optionally, roll a roulette over the back of the tile to give it texture.

8. Remove any imperfections in the pressed tile with a rubber-tipped cleaning tool or a small pencil eraser.

Demonstration 4: Using Props: Picture Frame

TOOLS & MATERIALS

Construction paper, long wooden stick, small wooden block, small knife, 45° triangle, brush & water, two slab boards, four ballast bags, stamps & roulettes

Ceramic frames give paintings and photographs an added measure of distinction. The broad face of this picture frame can be left mostly smooth with just some accent trim applied with a roulette, or it can be filled to the edges with imprints, appliqués and inscriptions. It is important to know how much the clay will shrink so the dimensions of the frame opening are correct after the frame has been fired. And, when fired, the frame needs special handling so it comes out as flat as it was when it went in.

1. Roll out a ⅜-in. thick slab on construction paper and smooth the surface. Lightly draw lines outlining the outside edges and opening of the frame. Decorate with textures, then cut the frame out. Keep all trimmings flat and in workable condition for use later.

2. The balance of the work is done with the picture frame face down. Use a pair of long, straight sticks to square up the sides and ends.

3. Square up the corners of the opening using a short block of wood.

4. Prepare eight 1-in. wide strips of clay from the slab trimmings.

From a Slab of Clay

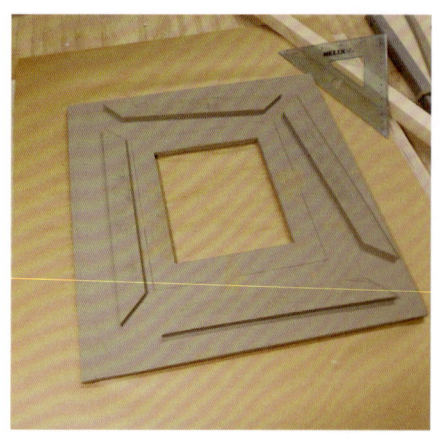

5. Create the inner frame from four strips. The inner frame should be ½ to 1 in. from the frame opening. Cut the strips at 45°.

6. Center and dry fit the strips then lightly draw lines around them to indicate where the frame needs to be scored and coated with slip.

7. Score and slip each inner frame piece and press into place using one of the sticks.

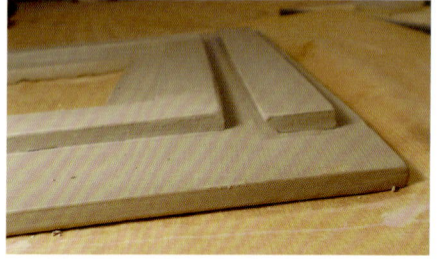

8. The frame hangs on a cleat strip made by cutting an angle into one of the strips. Score and attach with slip just below its top edge.

9. Lay the remaining three strips along the edge of the frame but do not attach. These remain with the frame through drying and firing to help it stay flat. Cover the frame with construction paper.

Demonstrations

10. Lay a slab board on top of the frame so slow drying can commence.

11. After a couple of days under the slab board, begin air drying the frame with its support strips beneath it and a ballast bag at each corner.

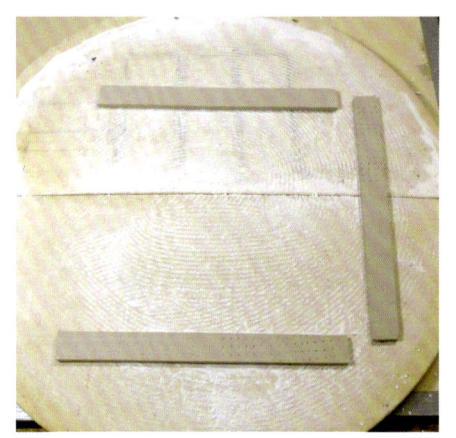

12. Coat kiln shelves with a thin layer of alumina hydrate to facilitate movement or of the frame and lay the bone-dry supports on the shelves.

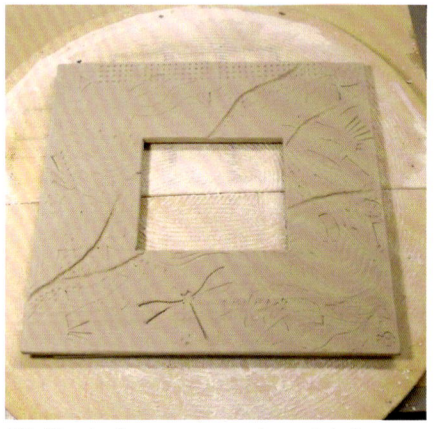

13. The dry frame on supports ready to fire.

From a Slab of Clay

Demonstration 5: Using a Slump Mold: Platter

TOOLS & MATERIALS
Paint edge trimmer, construction paper, shallow plastic platter, water-filled spray bottle, small knife, needle tool, dry cleaning bag (2), paint stir sticks (4), ballast bag, popsicle stick with shaped end

Traditionally, platters have been made by laying a large slab of clay into a large, shallow mold and trimming the edge in the same way the excess dough is trimmed from the crust of a pie. This demonstration presents an alternative approach—the slab is trimmed and its edge finished before it's placed in the mold, and all of the decorating is done while the slab lays flat on the table.

1. Roll out a slab of clay on construction paper just under ½ inch thick. Spray water on the surface and smooth it.

2. Place the platter form upside down on the slab and use a needle tool to cut out the shape from the slab.

3. Lightly drape a dry cleaning bag over the trimmed slab and carefully place the right-side up platter on the plastic, guided by your fingers.

4. Once you have the correct alignment, press the platter evenly on all sides to imprint the tray's oval foot in the clay.

Demonstrations

5. The area between the foot imprint and the edge of the slab defines the area to decorate. Lay plastic on the clay before pressing stamps.

6. Smooth the rim with your fingers then with tapered tip of a Popsicle stick. Lay a piece of plastic in the platter form.

7. Lift the decorated slab with a pair of paint stirring sticks in each hand and transfer it to the plastic-covered tray and carefully align it.

8. Cover the slab with another dry cleaning bag and use a ballast bag to form the slab to the platter mold.

9. With plastic in place, smooth rim with thumb and forefinger using a little downward pressure to seat the edge in the mold. Dry slowly.

10. Coat kiln shelf with a little alumina hydrate or silica to reduce the risk of cracking. Leave 2 inches of space above to assure even heating.

75

From a Slab of Clay

Demonstration 6: Using Slump Molds: Dishes

TOOLS & MATERIALS
Plastic trays (preferably two or three of the same size and shape), small paint brush, shaker of corn starch, dry cleaning bag or equivalent, texture stamps and roulettes

Small plastic trays containing microwaveable food come in a variety of shapes and sizes. With a little preparation these can be used as slump molds for quickly making a collection of dishes and trays.

1. Stack three identical food trays together to create a rigid mold. Lightly dust the top tray with corn starch and spread it evenly.

2. Roll out a ¼- to ⅜-in. thick slab about 25% larger than the mold and decorate it with stamps and roulettes. Carefully coax it into the tray.

3. Lay a dry cleaning bag over the clay to make it easier to press into the corners of the mold. This also helps protect the textures.

4. Trim some but not all of the excess clay. Tuck and smooth the edges to give it a more finished look without losing the freeform shape.

Demonstrations

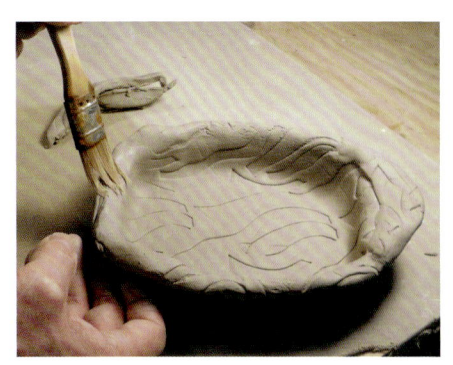

5. Fashion handles from scrap pieces and attach with slip. Additional texture is applied to each handle.

Examples of three pieces made from plastic microwave slump molds. The wall pocket on the left utilizes half a form attached to a clay slab (see Demonstration 7).

Using the Slump 'N Bump

6. The Slump 'N Bump mold is made by North Star and composed of four beveled sides held together with two rubber bands giving it flex.

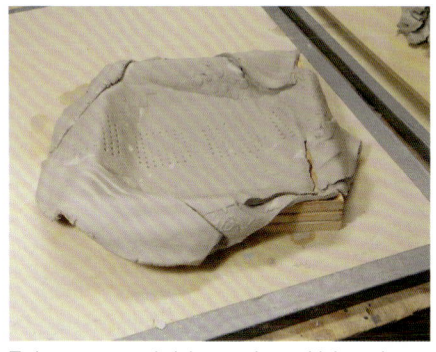

7. Lay a textured slab over the mold then place the mold and clay on the supplied bat. Texture both sides and add layers as desired.

8. Drop the bat with mold from waist height to the floor to force the clay deeply into the mold. The mold's sharp edges cleave off most of the excess clay. After trimming, add additional elements, then loosely cover to set up.

An example of a platter made using a Slump 'N Bump mold.

77

From a Slab of Clay

Demonstration 7: Using Press Molds: Wall Pocket

TOOLS & MATERIALS

Styrofoam food tray, small knife or needle tool, corn starch, sponge, brush, texture mat (optional), rolling pin & stack sticks or a slab roller, serrated rib, small rubber ball or ballast bag, Popsicle stick

This is a fun project that can be finished a variety of ways. Wall pockets can be used indoors or out. A small Styrofoam food tray serves as both a template and a mold for this two-part project.

1. Roll out two small slabs just under a ½-in. thick. Lay the meat tray face down on the slab and use a needle tool to cut around it.

2. Smooth the edge of the slab with your finger and set the slab aside.

3. Roll out a second slab the same size and sprinkle it with cornstarch. Use a dry brush to spread the cornstarch over the surface.

4. Press a texture mat firmly onto the slab. Use a rolling pin on the back of the mat to ensure a good imprint in the clay.

Demonstrations

5. Place the textured side face down in the meat tray. Coax the slab into the tray without overly stretching it or flattening out the texture.

6. Trim away the excess clay with a needle tool following the edge of the meat tray template.

7. Smooth the inside edge of the pocket with a rolling pin then make a straight cut across the tray to remove approximately 1/3 of the clay and give the pocket a nice top edge. Let the pocket remain in the meat tray to set up to leather-hard.

8. Once the back slab of the wall pocket is firm, use a stick with a sharp, beveled tip to gouge out two notches in the back. Both notches are made along a line drawn in the clay to ensure the wall pocket is level when hung on two nails.

9. Score edge of back slab where pocket will be placed, then slip. Score and slip the inside edge of the pocket, then press the parts together. Pack a paper towel in the pocket for support.

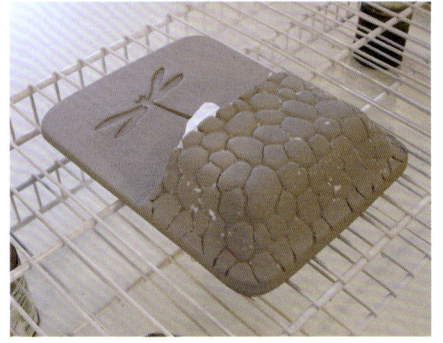

10. Place the wall pocket on a drying rack. At the leather-hard stage remove the paper towel and drill small drainage holes in the bottom of the pocket if it is intended to hold a live plant.

From a Slab of Clay

Demonstration 8: Making & Using Templates: Bowl

TOOLS & MATERIALS FOR THE DISH:
Small 1x4 block of wood with one end cut at a 45° angle, pencil, needle tool, fettling knife, rolling pin, serrated rib, small sponge, marking pen, drafting compass, X-Acto knife and #11 blades, 12x12-in. matte board or equivalent.

A template is useful when you want to make several items the same size and shape. The template for a dish looks something like a donut with a bite taken out of it, and the template for a pitcher is essentially the portion represented by the bite, albeit on a larger scale.

1. To see what form a flat template makes, cut a series of circles and experiment. Here the templates on the left and right produce different shaped truncated cones.

2. Draw an 11-in. circle on cardboard with a 5-in. circle in the center of it. Draw a right angle from the center to the edge and cut out the pieces with an X-Acto knife.

3. Lay the template on a slab of clay and trace around it. Remove the template and decorate the slab with stamps or drawn lines. Cut the arc.

4. Bevel the ends at 45° as well as the inside radius. When beveling the ends of the arc, bevel in opposite directions so the ends overlap.

Demonstrations

5. Score the edges, apply slip and bring the ends together to draw the shape up to form the wall of the bowl. Smooth the seam.

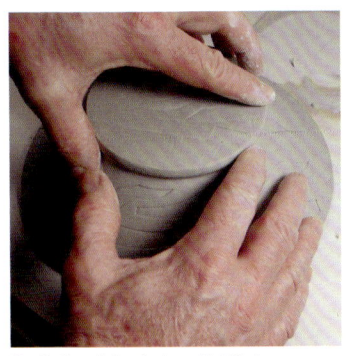

6. Cut a disk of clay slightly larger than the bottom opening of the dish to make a base. Decorate it and attach it with slip.

7. Finish the edge with a rounded stick and place decorative elements over the seam if you wish. Clean up any rough spots with a small brush and water.

Finished slab-built bowls created with a template.

81

From a Slab of Clay

Demonstration 9: Using Templates: Pitcher

TOOLS & MATERIALS
Small 1x4-in. block of wood with one end cut at a 45° angle, pencil, needle tool, fettling knife, rolling pin, serrated rib, small sponge, marking pen, X-Acto knife, poster board.

Both the dish and the pitcher are truncated cones, or simply cones with their points cut off. Templates are the best way to make several items the same size and shape, but finding the size you want is best done by trial and error.

1. For a 10-in. tall pitcher, secure template material to a piece of drywall, Using a string and pencil, draw an arc with a 24-in. radius and a second arc with an 13½-in. radius.

2. Mark the center of the arcs and draw a centerline for reference. Next, stretch the string taut and mark both arcs 15° to either side of the centerline.

3. Creating a cardboard mockup can give you an idea of how your form will look before you commit it to clay.

4. Cut out the template then transfer the design to roofing felt but add ¼ inch to ¾ inch on one edge to allow for overlapping at the seam.

82

Demonstrations

5. Roll out a slab of clay and lay the template on it. Use a needle tool to cut out the shape.

6. Apply slip to one edge and form the clay into a cone. Join the edges with equal overlap from top to bottom then smooth it with your fingers.

7. Cut out a small disk to use for the base. Wipe the excess slip away with a small brush.

8. Form the spout directly opposite the seam. Use a sponge and water to moisten the clay in this area afterward.

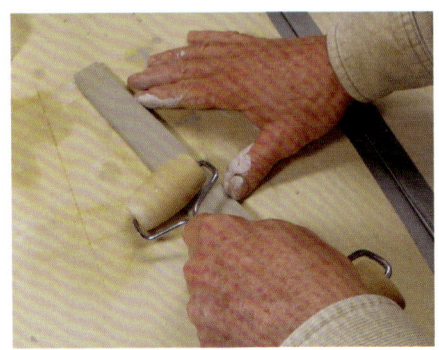

9. Cut a 10-in. long thin strip of clay for the pitcher's handle. Taper the edges with the pony roller and allow it to stiffen slightly.

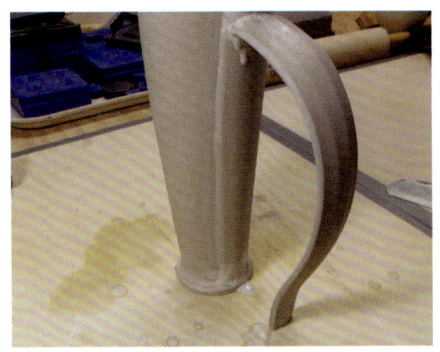

10. Score and slip across from the center of the beak where the handle will be attached, then press the top of the handle into place.

From a Slab of Clay

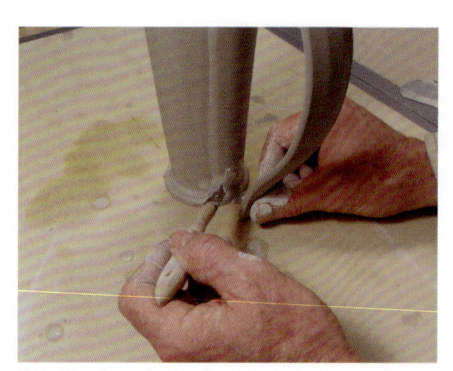

11. Check again for alignment then press the bottom of the handle into place. Smooth both joints and remove excess slip with a brush.

12. Prop the handle with a cardboard tube and a ruler until its shape is set.

The completed pitcher. Edges were rounded during construction using a notched wood tool then a leaf appliqué was added as decoration.

Demonstrations

Demonstration 10: Using Drape Forms: Sculpture

TOOLS & MATERIALS

Rolling pin, texture mats, stamps and roulettes, the pitcher template, a 16-in. length of a 3-in. diameter cardboard tube and two 2-in. dia. cardboard tubes (about 6 inches long); a rolling pin rest or two blocks of wood, two 18x24-in. sheets of construction paper, needle tool, fettling knife.

A slab can be cut and draped over a form in such a way that it can be used as the basis for a free-standing sculpture, like those made by Pacific Northwest artist Bill Klein. This is a soft slab project allowing for the attachment of parts with minimal scoring and light application of slip.

1. Roll out a 14-in. slab on construction paper that's a little less than ½-in. thick. Roll two different texture mats brushed with cornstarch into the slab, leaving the center portion smooth.

2. Lift the texture mats off and, using a template similar to the one used for the pitcher, cut an arc across the base, perpendicular to the centerline.

3. Trim the sides and set aside for later use. The trimmed slab should be 10 inches across at its widest point.

4. For the drape form, use a heavy-duty cardboard tube placed on a rolling pin rest or between blocks of wood.

85

From a Slab of Clay

5. Drape the trimmed slab over the form, center it and remove the paper backing. Hold a drawing of the wing next to the body to judge the fit, then cut out the wing pattern.

6. Texture clay slabs then cut them out using the template. Use light slip to attach both wings. Press them firmly into place then wipe away the excess slip. Use a tube to prop each wing.

7. Freehand cut the beak from a textured slab and attach it. Cut semicircles from a textured slab for use above the eyes.

9. The finished sculpture needs to firm up before being lifted off of the drape form. With all of its attached parts, slow drying is essential.

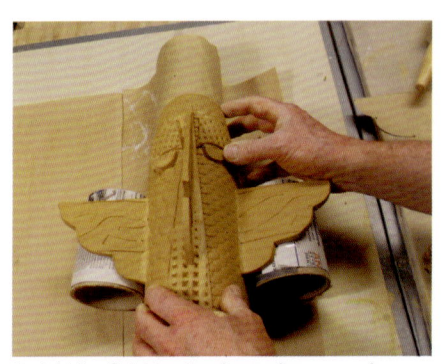

8. Add the finishing touches using more pieces cut from the textured trimmings. Brush water on pieces and press them into place.

Demonstrations

Demonstration 11: Joining Slabs: Lidded Box

TOOLS & MATERIALS
Two small blocks of wood, slip, small brush, needle tool or small knife, rubber-tipped clean-up tool. Optional: a small banding wheel, Surform tool.

The ceramic box is one of the most time-honored demonstrations of the handbuilder's skill. It requires careful planning, measuring, cutting and fitting. This is the first of two demonstrations. In this demo, a box is made where the joints are butted together, and then in the next demonstration, a box is made using mitered joints.

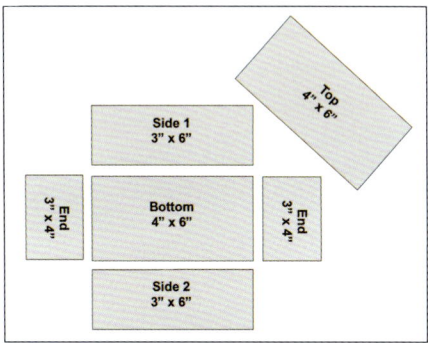

1. Roll out a ⅜-in. thick slab and cut pieces according to the diagram when soft leather-hard. Wrap the leftover pieces for later use.

2. Trim the two end pieces by twice the thickness of the slab, e.g., if the slab is ⅜-in. thick, cut ¾-in. off of each end piece.

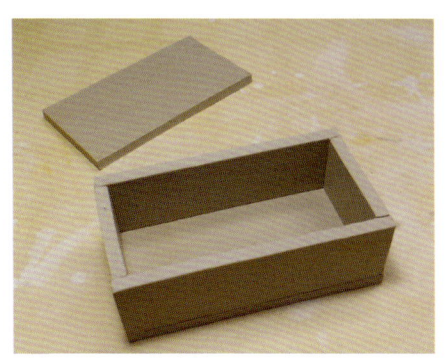

3. Dry fit the pieces without slip to be sure the box will go together correctly.

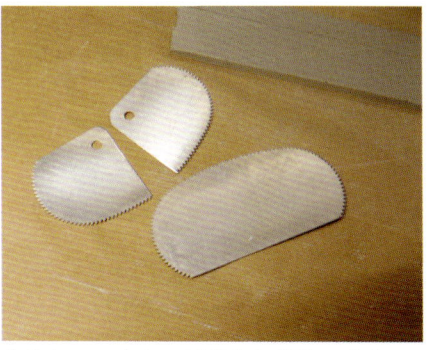

4. Cut a serrated metal rib in half. Smooth the corners and use them for precise scoring.

87

From a Slab of Clay

5. Dry fit the base and side pieces then score all the edges where pieces meet. Coat with slip then assemble.

6. Use two small wood blocks to square up the box and press the joints together. Use a brush to spread excess slip and to smooth interior seams.

7. Score the top and attach it with slip. Use a block of wood again to firmly attach the top to the rest of the box.

8. Wipe excess slip from the outside of the box and smooth the seams.

9. Make an even cut all the way around the box ¾ in. from the top using a small knife. Use a rubber-tipped tool to smooth the interior seam.

10. Roll leftover scraps to half their thickness then cut and trim the side and end pieces for the box's gallery to length.

88

Demonstrations

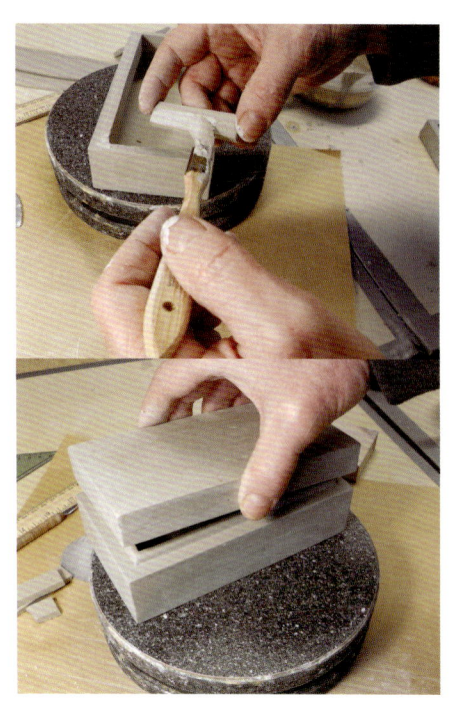

Tip: Wrap a small piece of paper around the box and secure it with three large rubber bands. Then, allow the box to dry upside down. This will reduce the risk of warping. Also bisque fire the box upside down.

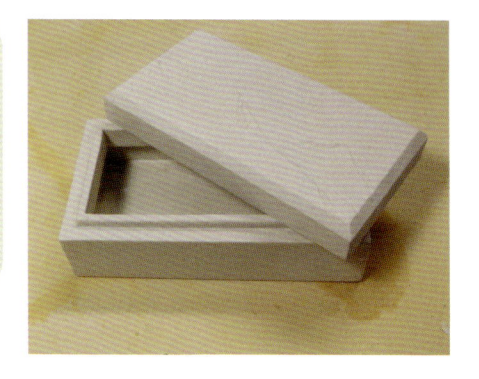

From a Slab of Clay

Demonstration 12: Joining Slabs: Mitered Box

TOOLS & MATERIALS

Carpenter's square or an 8x10-inch picture frame, 45° triangle, two or three wood blocks to use as props, serrated rib, construction paper or building paper, two wood paddles, sponge, pony roller, small knife, small brush, resist wax, rubber mallet, and the miter press tool (described below).

The second box is made using mitered joints. Miters have a large surface area that makes a strong joint, but cutting them on clay slabs often proves frustrating for all but the most practiced hands. A six-sided box having all mitered joints requires 24 of these beveled edges, so a simpler, faster way of making them is demonstrated here.

1. The "miter press" tool consists of a length of 1x4 lumber with two 45° cuts made on one end to make a point. The model here is made from pine although a harder wood is recommended.

2. Two miter presses are shown here—one 18-in. long and one 8-in. long. Sections of a yardstick have been attached to each with screws. The miter presses will be used later.

3. Roll out a 20-in. slab that's ½-in. thick slab on a piece of building paper. Lightly scribe six 6x6-in. squares from the slab.

4. Hold the 18-in. miter press vertically over one of the outermost grid lines and use a rubber mallet to make the first mitered cut.

Demonstrations

5. Use the 8-in miter press to clean up the cuts and make sure the pieces are cut all the way through.

6. Allow the six sides of the box to firm up so that each can be lifted from the paper without flexing.

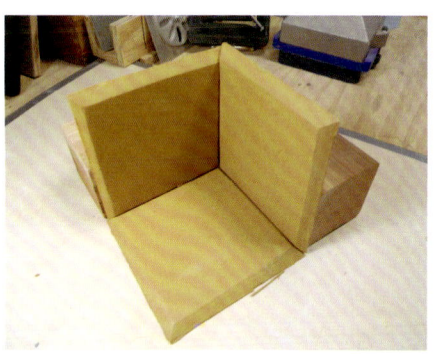

7. Dry fit the six sides and support them with wood blocks. Check the fit then disassemble.

8. Place the box's base on a smaller piece of construction paper and score the edges. The same is done for each of the other sides.

9. Prepare slip from your clay body then slip all edges at once or one at a time. Use a triangle to be sure the sides are vertical as you build.

10. After the fourth side is in place, reinforce the interior seams with small coils of fresh clay. Smooth the joints with your fingers.

From a Slab of Clay

11. Check the box to be sure it is square on all sides then attach the top. Use a damp sponge to smooth all of the joints.

12. Use wood blocks to strengthen the joints on all sides.

13. Smooth and square the seams with your thumbs, or use a pony roller.

14. Having the box on paper makes it easier to lift so it can be rotated to work on the other sides.

15. Wrap the box snuggly with plastic and allow it sit overnight before continuing.

16. The next day, cut the lid freehand with a small knife. The undulating cut helps the lid stay in place when resting on top of the box.

Demonstrations

17. Clean the edges of the cut with the knife and a clean-up tool then replace the lid and smooth the outside edges so the lid will have a nice fit.

18. Coat the rim of the box and lid with wax resist to help both sections dry without warping. Since the box is sealed shut, poke a small hole in the box to release trapped air.

19. Use a Surform tool to bevel the top and bottom edges, then lightly wrap the piece in plastic to start the drying process.

A completed box made from mitered parts using the preceding technique.

From a Slab of Clay

Demonstration 13: Using Forms: Tankard

TOOLS & MATERIALS
Rolling pin, pony roller, construction paper or building paper, serrated rib, slip and small brush, a paper tube (3-in. dia.), a paper tube (2-in. dia. or smaller), circle cutter or disk cutter, disposable chopstick or other long stick, banding wheel.

The tankard, or tall cup, is made from one slab of clay from which three components are cut: the slab that will be rolled up to become the body, a disk used for the base and a strap for the cup's handle. Once the basics are mastered, there are many ways a cup can be individualized.

1. Prepare a ¼-in. thick about 14-in. in dia. Texture the slab using texture rollers before cutting the pieces.

2. Cut the slab for the cylinder. Multiply the diameter of the tube by 3.14 (π) and add twice the thickness of the clay to one end. Taper one end and one side. Leave the other end square.

3. Flip the slab over and taper the other end and also the side previously tapered. The double-tapered side becomes the rim of the tankard.

4. Score and slip one tapered end of the slab then flip it over and repeat on the other tapered end on the textured side.

Demonstrations

5. With both ends prepared, roll the slab, textured side out, into a cylinder using a small tube for support.

6. Carefully align the slip-coated tapered ends and lightly press them together so they can be repositioned, if necessary.

7. Stand the cylinder on end and insert the 3-in. tube. Adjust the overlap and press the seam together.

8. Once the shape is set, withdraw the tube and smooth the inner and outer seams. Note the taper of the rim in this photo.

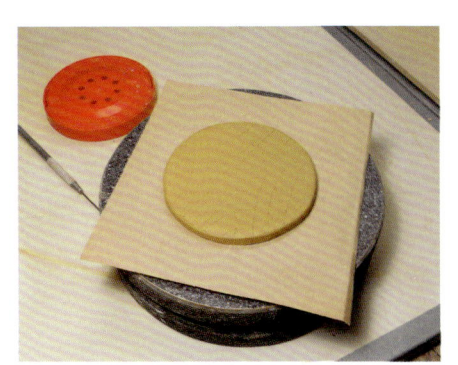

9. Use a disk cutter (this one from the top of a soup can) to cut out a disk slightly larger than the diameter of the tankard body.

10. Score and slip the bottom edge of the tankard body.

95

From a Slab of Clay

11. Score and slip the edge of the disk and press the body into place.

12. Reinsert the paper tube to restore the shape of the body.

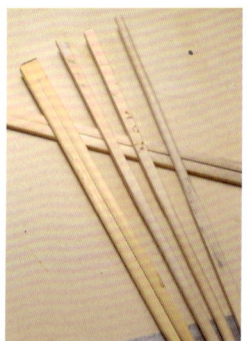

13. Sticks, such as these chopsticks, are useful for cleaning the seams in tall shapes. They can be used as they are or shaped.

14. Use a small stick to refine the shape of the tankard's base. Later it will be lifted and smoothed with a damp sponge.

15. For a handle, add texture to a clay strip. Attach the handle directly over the seam and support it with a small paper tube until set.

Finished tankards ready for beverage.

Demonstrations

Demonstration 14: The One-Slab Pitcher

TOOLS & MATERIALS
Paint edge trimmer, needle tool, 3-in. dia. paper tube (24 in. long), 2-in. stack of newspapers, serrated rib, brush & water, popsicle stick, ballast bag or small rubber ball, pony roller, pizza cutter, small knife and sponge.

This demonstration illustrates how some projects require props during construction rather than just at the end during drying. In the case of the one-slab pitcher, a stack of newspapers is needed as a prop under the slab while it is being made. The pitcher will be more than 15 inches tall when finished so it has to be created from a slab at least 22 inches in diameter.

1. Cut a slab measuring 5 inches at it widest point using a straightedge and needle tool. The cut piece will be used later for the pitcher's base.

2. For the part of the slab that will become the pitcher's handle to be centered, use a 1-in. thick stack of newspapers under it.

3. Loosely wrap newspaper around a paper tube and tape it. With the slab partially resting on the newspaper stack, lay the paper tube on the slab.

4. With the tube even with the cut edge of clay, roll the slab over it and lightly press into place, taking care not to mar the slab with your fingers.

From a Slab of Clay

5. Use a ballast bag to mold the slab around the paper tube.

6. Use a pony roller to make a good seal where the slab has been folded onto itself.

7. Move the newspaper stack to the left side and roll the slab over onto it.

8. Roll and press this side just as you did the first side. Lightly draw shape of the handle and use a pizza cutter to trim away the excess.

9. Slip a small, thin board under the handle. Round the bottom half of the handle with a tapered Popsicle stick.

10. Cut the inner area of the handle with a small knife or needle tool and lift it out.

Demonstrations

11. With the paper tube still inside, stand the pitcher on the slab cut off in the first step. Trace the outside of the pitcher's body, including the handle onto the slab with a needle tool.

12. Cut the bottom slightly oversized (about ½ inch wider than the pitcher). Carefully lay the pitcher on its side and score and slip the bottom. Attach the body with firm downward pressure.

13. Smooth the seam between the body and the bottom piece with your fingers.

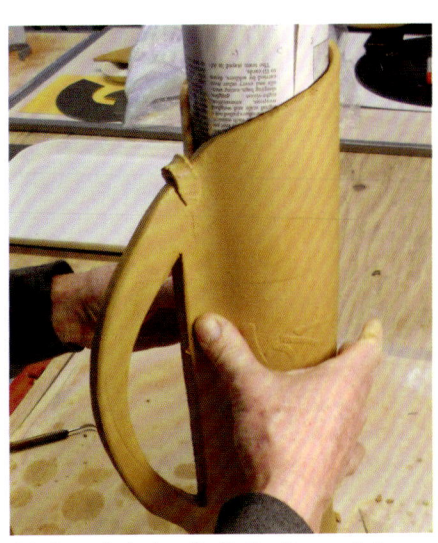

14. Smooth the handle. Notice the small strap of clay applied at the top of the handle. This is decorative but also helps control splitting.

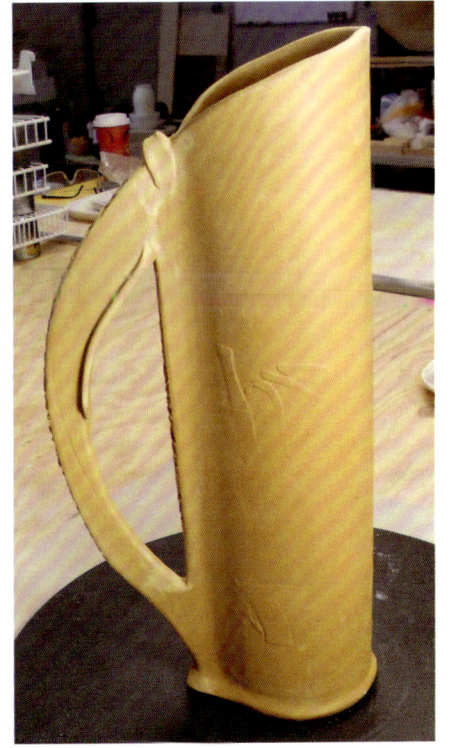

15. With the paper tube in place, trim the rim with a small knife, remove the tube then smooth the rim. Clean the interior using a long stick. Add a small strip of clay where the pitcher will be grasped. This helps minimize the risk of splitting. Wrap the pitcher for slow, controlled drying.

99

From a Slab of Clay

Demonstration 15: Adding Texture: Free-form Bowl

TOOLS & MATERIALS

Dry cleaning bag, texture-makers including texture mats, brushes, colored slips, lace doily, a 15-in. wok or bowl, ballast bag, support blocks (4) cut from a 4x4 post

Even though this is a free-form bowl, it requires a methodical approach and the use of a few tricks along the way so it makes it through the rigors of firing in beautiful shape. The starting slab is 20 inches in diameter and rolled to about ¼-in. thick, making it thinner than most of the other project slabs. However, several slab pieces are going to be added so the bowl will gain weight along with its distinctive look.

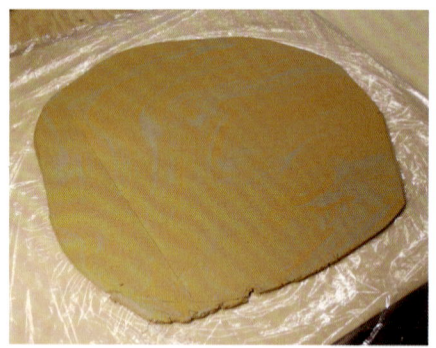

1. Roll out a ¼-in. thick slab about 20 inches in diameter and place it on a thin piece of plastic (dry cleaning bag).

2. Decorate the center area with stamps or rollers. Here, a roller used for tenderizing meat is used.

3. Brush on slip then arrange torn pieces of slabs using enough pressure to bond them to the slab without disturbing the texture in the center.

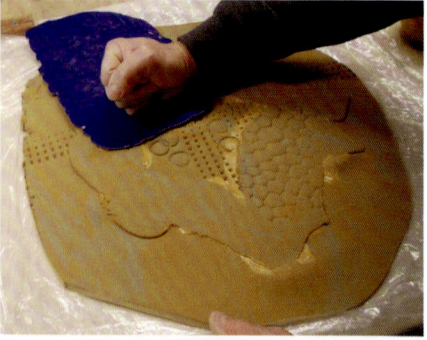

4. Here a texture mat is used to give the torn pieces their own texture, but anything from the "texture arsenal" can be tried.

100

Demonstrations

5. Brush a contrasting colored slip on the textured pieces.

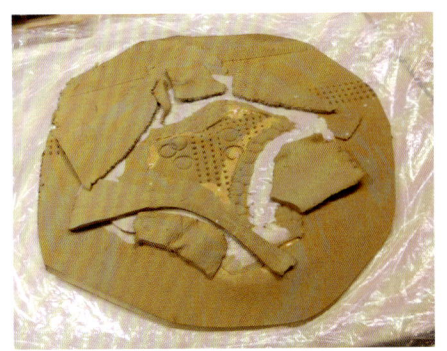

6. Press more pieces into place, decorate with textures and add more colored slips using using a brush or sponge to highlight the textures.

7. The slab is ready to be placed in the bowl, which in this case is an old cooking wok with its handles cut off.

8. The multi-layered slab is still very flexible, so lift it by the plastic and lay it into the bowl.

9. Coax the slab into the bowl. While the bowl is rotated, lift the slab and plastic at the edges to help the slab move deeper into the bowl.

10. Use a ballast bag to press the slab into the bowl. Fold over the plastic sheet to keep the ballast bag from smearing the slip.

From a Slab of Clay

11. Trim overhanging clay from the edge of the bowl, and set it aside to possibly work into the design later.

12. Use a dry brush to spread the slip into recessed areas.

13. Either tuck in the clay at the bowl's rim or fold it over. Texture and attach pieces trimmed earlier. Cover with plastic and allow it to set up overnight. Remove when leather-hard.

14. Remove the plastic and set the bowl on drywall to dry. Use four wooden blocks to support the bowl.

Demonstration 16: Using Drape Molds: Bowl

TOOLS & MATERIALS FOR THE MOLD

12-in. dia. plastic bowl, pottery plaster & plaster mixing tools, three 5-in. angle brackets. Optional: 15- or 16-in. pottery wheel bat, (3) ¼ x 1-in. flathead machine screws, (3) locking washers, (3) ¼ in. hex nuts, drill & ¼ in. bit for drilling holes in the bat.

TOOLS & MATERIALS FOR THE BOWL

Assorted stamps & roulettes, pony roller, a plastic cup (the rim of which is slightly smaller than the diameter of the bowl's base), pencil or pointed stick, rib or small knife, level, a 10 x 10-in. piece of Masonite (or equivalent).

As we've shown, bowls and dishes can be formed by pressing slabs into molds. Here, a bowl is formed by pressing it onto a mold. First, the mold, itself, is made, and then two different ways to use it are shown.

HOW TO MIX PLASTER

Add plaster to water

Use a clean plastic bucket for mixing plaster. Always add plaster to water, not the other way around. The plaster-to-water ratio by weight is 10:7, for example, add ten pounds of plaster to seven pounds of water. Weigh your plaster first, then multiply that weight by 0.7 to find the weight of the water. By volume: Add 2¾ lbs. of plaster to a quart of water. Use cool or room temperature plaster and water. Never use hot water.

Let the mix rest

Let the mixed plaster sit (slake) for one to two minutes before stirring. For small batches of 5 lbs. or less, a minute may be enough.

Stir the mix

Mix the plaster by hand or with a power mixer. Mix smaller batches (under 10 lbs. of plaster) for two minutes. Larger batches require a longer mixing time, e.g., a mix of 25 lbs. of plaster needs 4 minutes. A power mixer should be used at the highest setting while moving it slowly around the batch to minimize trapping air bubbles.

From a Slab of Clay

Wait before pouring

After mixing, tap the side of the bucket vigorously to encourage the escape of air bubbles. Stir slowly to feel the mix beginning to stiffen slightly and when the plaster has lost some of its shine it's ready to pour. Once the plaster mix is in the mold, tap the sides gently to settle the plaster.

Let the plaster set up

The plaster will gradually harden and it will feel warm to the touch. In about 30 minutes the plaster can be removed from the mold.

Dry the mold

The mold has to dry completely before use. Depending on the thickness of the mold and the environment in which it is drying, this will take a week or more. It is best to allow the plaster to dry at its own pace rather than attempting to accelerate it. Temperatures above 125°F will damage the plaster.

1. Prepare plaster and pour it into plastic bowl to roughly the half-way mark. While the plaster is still viscous, insert the angle brackets with the spacing as shown. The end of each bracket should rest on the rim of the bowl. Work quickly to level the brackets using a board or level.

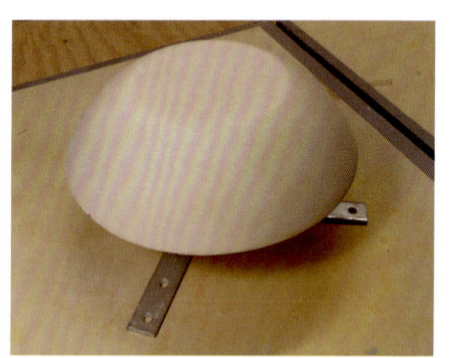

2. Remove the bowl after an hour. Run a knife around the edge to remove the sharp rim. Allow the mold to dry for 5-7 days. Do not force dry in an oven or a kiln.

Demonstrations

3. To determine how big your slab needs to be, use a measuring tape to check the width of the mold.

4. Roll out a ⅜-in. thick slab on a sheet of construction paper and decorate it with stamps.

5. Lift the slab with the paper and flip it onto the mold. Gently smooth it with your hand, then trim excess clay from the edge using a knife.

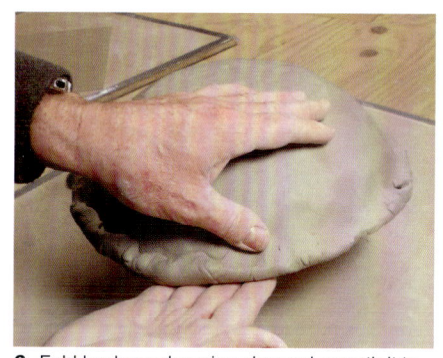

6. Fold back overhanging clay and smooth it to create a free-form rim.

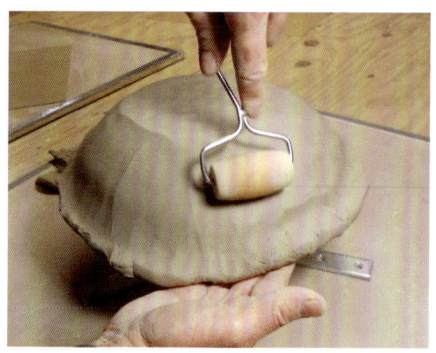

7. Use the large end of a pony roller to flatten the bowl's base, and the small end to smooth down the sides of the bowl.

8. Create a repeating pattern by holding the roulette at the same angle with each stroke. Changing the angle and flipping the roulette yields a random pattern.

From a Slab of Clay

9. Add a couple of handles made from the still-soft trimmings and continue working on the rim.

10. Mark the location of the foot.

11. Lay a coil on the traced line and trim the excess. Overlap the ends and slice through the middle of the overlap. Press the ends of the coil together and smooth the join.

12. Shape and compress the coil with your fingers and a couple of small spoons (optional).

13. Press a pony roller into the foot in three places to add visual interest.

14. Place a piece of construction paper over the foot and set a bat on it. Apply downward pressure with a bubble level until the foot is trued up in all directions.

Demonstrations

15. Allow the bowl to firm up overnight then lift it from the form. Wipe the interior edge of the rim smooth and move it to a drying rack.

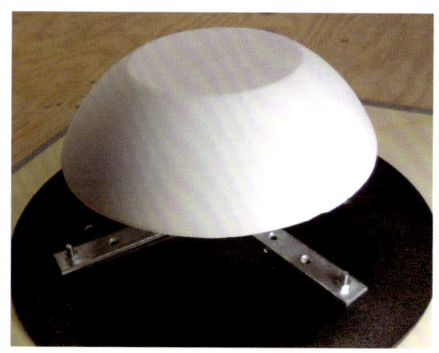

16. To use the mold on a pottery wheel, center the mold and mark the location, then drill mounting holes to attach it to the bat with ¼x1-in. flathead machine screws and nuts.

17. Carefully press a slab over the mold. As the wheel spins, trim excess clay and apply texture with a roulette. Add and throw a ring of clay for a footring.

18. Remove the bowl the next day and finish the rim using a profile tool.

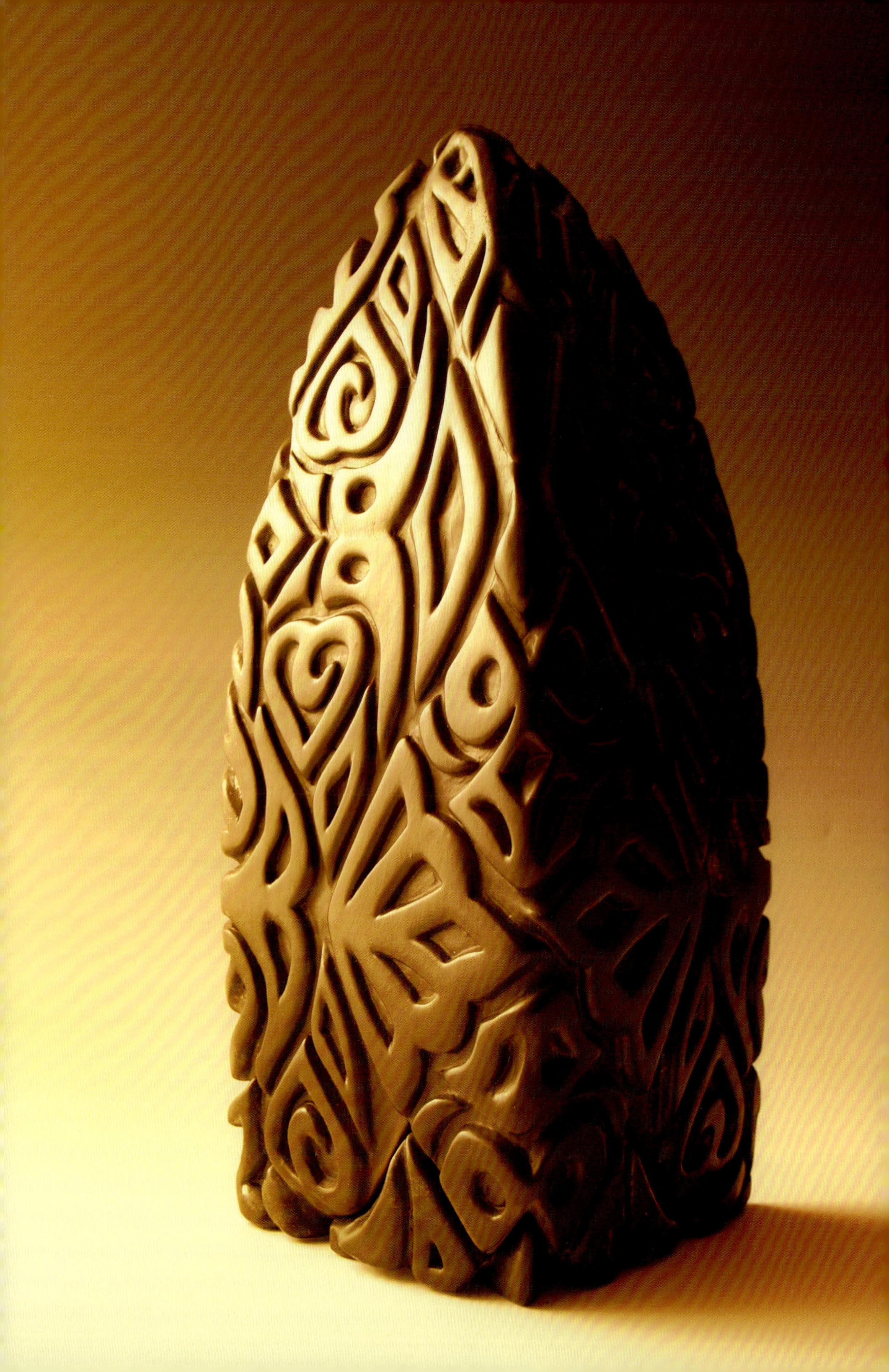

CHAPTER **6**

Drying, Firing and Glazing Considerations

Even the simplest slab project represents an investment of time and energy so it's important that each project survives the firing process. The quality of construction, that is, how well you make each piece, cannot be overemphasized. In short, if you build it, dry it and load it into your kiln correctly, it increases your chances for it to fire correctly. But, build it haphazardly or ignore proper procedures and you will likely face pottery that is warped, cracked, or worse when you open your kiln.

Slow Drying

Part and parcel of quality slab construction is proper drying. Generally speaking, your clay projects shouldn't be subjected to firing until they are completely dry. Clay may appear to be dry, and it may even feel dry to the touch, yet it can retain moisture. In the early firing stage, at 212°F (100°C), moisture turns to steam that needs to find its way out of the clay. Without an easy path, the pressure can build and the result can be explosive. So, how do you know when a piece of clay is dry enough to go in your kiln? If you can't trust the touch of your fingers, then trust a more sensitive part of your body. Hold the object to your cheek. If the piece has lost its coolness, then it's probably ready for the kiln. With experience, you'll know the nature of the clay and how much moisture it can retain before it can be fired.

Methods and Materials

Robert Piepenburg and, no doubt, many others, refer to the slow drying process as babysitting—doting over a project up to the point where it's consigned to the kiln. As a rule, more of this babysitting is required for large-scale projects and particularly for those where several pieces of clay have been connected. There are only a few basic items necessary to equip your work area so you can control the drying of your projects.

Thin plastic. Dry cleaning bags are essential. They're large enough to completely cover most any project and soft enough to rest on the surface of the clay without marring it.

Tabletop sculpture, brushed with terra sigilatta at the bone dry stage, bisque fired to cone 06 and black fired to cone 012, by Rose Bauer, ht: 12 in.

Plastic shopping bags. Cheap grocery stores bags are comparatively coarse and are more suited for short-term storage of clay scraps than for controlled drying.

Newspaper. Setting a project on two or three sheets of newspaper is an excellent way to control the drying of the underside of a project. Where clay placed directly on a wooden board is at risk of over drying, newsprint under the clay absorbs the moisture to the point of saturation, allowing you to remove it and replace it with dry sheets.

Rubber bands. A variety of sizes come in very handy for securing the plastic wrap around your work.

Masking tape. When rubber bands won't suffice, masking tape will work. The blue, "painter's tape" can be removed from plastic wrap with less damage.

Elastic Bandage. As mentioned, this is handy for supporting pieces after assembly, but it's also useful for holding dry cleaning bags or other plastic wrap snuggly in place around a piece during drying.

Wax resist. This can be used to slow the drying where two pieces of clay have been joined, thereby reducing the risk of cracking. The lid can be sealed onto a clay box with the wax throughout drying to reduce warping. Wax resist is sold by the pint, quart or gallon at any pottery supply store.

Grog or fine sand. As clay dries it shrinks and moves slightly. Placing a large-scale project, like a platter or large tile, on a "sand sandwich" allows it to move during drying and lessens the risk of warping or cracking. To make, spread a layer of fine-mesh sand or grog between two sheets of newspaper.

Plastic bucket. Inverting a 5-gallon plastic bucket over a work-in-progress will bring drying to almost a full stop and the surface of the clay won't be touched at all.

Styrofoam cooler. This, with its fitted lid, can be used as an inexpensive "damp box" for maintaining the condition of the clay. A moist sponge placed in a plastic cup inside the closed cooler helps maintain the humidity. The cooler's lid can be removed for interval drying.

Drywall. Two-foot square pieces of drywall are essential for drying flat work. In all but the most humid of climates, drywall dries quickly and stays flat so that, if saturated, it can be flipped and put back into use.

Ballast bags. Completely flat projects can be sandwiched between sheetrock for drying but tiles with raised surface elements need ballast bags to help them stay flat. They're easy to make and it's a good idea to have several on hand in a variety of sizes and weights.

Spray bottle. It's a good idea to have two or three spray bottles on hand as they have a way of wandering out of reach or of being misplaced altogether. Work in progress can be sprayed directly or the interior of a storage container can be sprayed to add humidity.

Accelerated Drying

While slow, controlled drying is the best way to prepare your projects for the kiln, the fact is that there are going to be times when you may not be able to babysit your projects as slowly as you'd like. You can rush it some, but it needs to be done carefully.

How to Make a Ballast Bag

Cut a piece of dry cleaning bag and lay it on a piece of cheesecloth or any soft cloth.

Place a small mound of dry sand in the center.

Draw up the corners without squeezing the sand too much. Secure bag with a twist tie.

Make several ballast bags to keep on hand.

Old wire refrigerator shelves stacked on small cans or blocks of wood make excellent drying racks. The free flow of air around the clay helps the clay dry evenly.

Sunshine. Have you ever noticed how warm the interior of your car is on a bright, sunny, but cold, day? This is the result of the sun's electromagnetic radiation warming the confined air. The same phenomenon can occur if clay work is placed in the sunshine inside a closed container. The interior of the container warms quickly and moisture in the clay will humidify the air in the container. By opening the container periodically the moisture can be released and the rate of drying can be controlled. Give extra attention to projects placed uncovered, directly in the sunshine; especially on very warm days. The exposed, upper surface tends to dry much faster than the lower surface and warping, curling or cracking may result. By rotating or flipping the clay frequently, the sun can be put to work for you very effectively.

Hair dryer. While not suitable for completely drying a project, a hair dryer is useful for firming up very moist clay during assembly. For instance, suppose you want to make cups from slabs you just rolled. With the hair dryer, both sides of each slab can be warmed until the surface tackiness is gone and the clay can be rolled without distorting the shape. The dryer can again be used to firm up the handles before attaching them.

Heat gun. This can quickly develop enough concentrated heat to soften, even blister, paint and isn't really of any practical use in clay work.

Kitchen oven. To use the oven to dry work in, stack work evenly in a cold oven using clay wads to aid air and heat circulation. Prop open the oven door slightly to allow moisture to escape, then bring the oven up to temperature slowly, at a rate no higher than 60°F per hour, to a target temperature below 212°F. Periodically remove a piece and allow it to cool slowly. Inspect it to determine how dry it is. If you deem the rest of the clay to be dry enough, then shut off the oven and allow it to cool until you can safely handle the pieces.

Electric Kiln. One of the most reliable ways to accelerate the drying of slab work is to preheat, or "candle" it, very slowly, in an electric kiln. To preheat clay in a manually operated kiln, follow the manufacturer's operating instructions for setting up the kiln for normal operation. Prop the kiln's lid open approximately 3 inches then turn the bottom knob to the lowest setting. If it's equipped with a limit timer, set it to 10 hours and start the kiln. Projects that are ¾–1-in. thick may require additional heating. Once the clay is completely dry, the normal firing routine can be followed. If you have a digital controller, use the Ramp/Hold function to set up the preheat routine. Typically, the controller is programmed to raise the kiln temperature at a rate of 60°F (38°C) per hour until the kiln reaches 180°F (82°C). Then the controller is programmed to hold the temperature for eight to ten hours, or longer, depending how wet and how thick the clay is. Propping the lid isn't necessary for kilns equipped with underside ventilation systems. If your kiln has a pre-heat function, select it prior to starting the normal firing routine. In later-model Skutt kilns, for instance, when the Cone Fire button is pressed the code "PRHT" appears on the controller's display and the preheat routine may be selected or bypassed. Consult your kiln's operation manual for additional instructions pertaining to the preheating your clay work.

Your Kiln and Firing Your Work

Your completely dry clay is now ready for its first firing. The bisque firing is where it will be transformed from brittle, water-soluble clay into pottery. A full tutorial on how to load and operate your kiln is beyond the scope of this book. However, there are several key points that are especially pertinent to firing hand-built pottery. Above all else, know your kiln and how to operate it. If you have the operation manual, study it thoroughly. If you don't have a manual, contact the manufacturer to see if they have a replacement copy. A manual may also be available for download from the manufacturer's website.

Learn how to assess the condition of the kiln and be able to detect any damage that can lead to malfunctions. Studio kilns are designed to be easy to maintain. Repair procedures, like

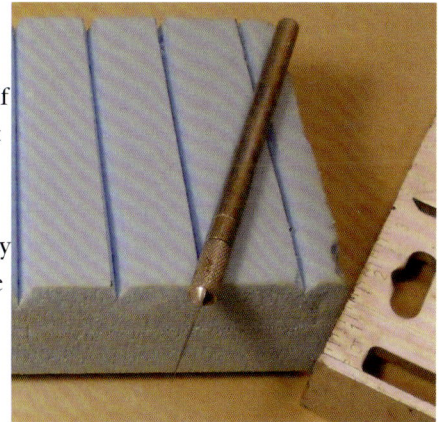

Styrofoam insulation panels can be cut into a variety of shapes and sizes. Cut grooves into them an inch apart so air can get underneath the slabs for drying.

heating element and brick replacement, are detailed in operation manuals.

Shelves and posts. Key components of the kiln are its shelves and posts; commonly referred to as kiln furniture. For flat slab work, such as tiles, platters, trays and masks, it's especially important that the shelves are flat and smooth. Glaze drips should be ground off and a fresh coat of kiln wash applied.

Props. If a piece needs to be stabilized during the firing, make props from your clay body as you make your piece and fire the piece supported by the props at the same time.

Waster slabs. These are slabs used under a project and any props to provide an even surface during the firing. The waster slab is made with the project and accompanies it through each firing.

Stilts. Generally speaking, stilts are used to elevate pottery that has been glazed on the underside.

The Complicated Approach

There are dozens of books and online resources that explain how and what you need to make your own glazes from scratch. Many who are just getting into glaze making will assemble only the tools, containers and raw materials needed to make a particular glaze from a recipe found in a book or online. With some early success they will add more tools, more containers and certainly more raw materials, guided by more recipes. Others who get disappointing results, early on, may sound the retreat and opt to use only pre-mixed glazes.

The Simpler Approach

Over the last fifteen years great strides have been made in the formulation and commercial production of pre-mixed pottery glazes. Pottery supply companies now offer hundreds of dry-mix and liquid glazes that eliminate the need to understand glaze recipes or to invest in various raw materials. Pre-mixed dry glazes have to be mixed with the correct proportion of water. Since some glaze components may not completely break down in water, you'll need to put the glaze through a glaze sieve and stir it to ensure that it's ready for use. Liquid glazes are sold in pint, quart and gallon containers, and may need to be thinned with water and stirred before being suitable for use. Experiment with both dry and liquid glazes. Layer or mix them to create even more glaze colors and textures.

Kiln Wash Tip

Sylvia Nagy of Brooklyn, New York has found that kiln wash made from a mixture of alumina hydrate and kaolin flakes off of shelves onto pottery when the shelves are flipped. Instead, Sylvia uses alumina hydrate mixed only with water. She brushes the mixture on her kiln shelves and, after firing, it becomes powder again. Cleaning is as easy as brushing the powder from the shelves. The alumina hydrate can be reclaimed, mixed with water again and reapplied to the shelves for the next firing. An added bonus is that the powder enables the ceramic pieces to move a bit during the firing, which cuts down on warping that may occur during shrinkage. This kiln wash is ideally suited for use in electric kilns where there is little to no air movement during firing.

If you plan to fire a large quantity of tiles, invest in tile setters. Each tile setter holds several tiles and they can be stacked on top of each other. Setters allow air to circulate around the tiles to help them dry and fire evenly.

Note: Just because you can fire your kiln fast, doesn't mean you should. A slow, metered rate of temperature climb can usually yield better results when firing an electric kiln.

Test, Test, Test! No matter which approach you take, and no matter how good the glaze you mixed up looks in a photo, on a jar label or even on someone else's fired pottery, you need to test it. First fire it on test pieces made from the same clay and constructed similarly to the pieces upon which you have worked so hard. For instance, if you've made several incised or embossed tiles, then your test pieces should be similarly incised or embossed. A glaze intended for use on press-molded dishes or cups shouldn't be tested on flat tiles placed horizontally in the kiln. Doing so might show the color and surface texture of the glaze, but it might cloak the fact that the glaze flows a great deal during firing. Your test pieces should be fired in exactly the same way you plan to fire your load of pieces. Bringing the glazing and firing variables under your control will significantly increase the value of your tests.

Variables that affect glazes

- Clay body color
- Clay maturity temperature (e.g., cone 6 - 10)
- Construction method (e.g., slab rolled, press molded)
- Clay decoration elements (embossed, impressed, carved)
- Object shape (e.g., tile, box, cylinder, sculpture)
- Highest temperature of bisque firing (e.g., cone 04)
- Glaze application method (e.g., brushed, dipped, sprayed)
- Glaze thickness (e.g., number of coats, times dipped, coats sprayed)
- Glaze sequence (i.e., the order of application if using multiple glazes on a piece)
- Glaze firing temperature (e.g., cone 6)

Finally, which comes first, the things you make from a slab of clay or the glaze? No doubt you said it's your "slabs d'art" that came first. But, consider this. As you build your glaze palette and become familiar with each glaze in it, what you make from clay and how you make it will be influenced by what you have in that glaze palette. Knowing you have one or more glazes that flow beautifully over raised marks and into imprints, will compel you to make more things with that sort of texture. Hence, you may find yourself saying, "I have this beautiful glaze, I think I will make an embossed vase to go under it," instead of saying, "I made this beautiful embossed vase, I wonder which glaze will look best on it." The former approach is likely to result in higher satisfaction and less disappointment than the latter.

Here's where our investigation of glazes and glaze development stops, but for you it may be just beginning. The best advice is to consult several of the pottery texts available at your local library or from booksellers. Also, trust the guidance you can receive from the staff members at pottery supply companies. Many of these good folks are potters themselves and they're always willing to share what they know about the glazes they sell.

CHAPTER 7

Gallery

Welcome. The works of artists displayed here all began as a slab of clay utilizing many of the same techniques illustrated in the "Demonstration" section of this book. There are pieces that started out flat and basically stayed that way—tiles, trays, platters and plates—and there are examples of bowls and cups. You'll also find several examples of boxes showing how different artists interpret this simple shape, as well as variations on bottles, vases, jars, and teapots. Here, the slab may stand tall and straight or spread out and undulate. Finally, sculptures by artists from North and South America as well as Australia reveal a range from representational to highly abstract showing the incredible versatility of a slab of clay.

Platter, slump molded and textured, slip decoration, salt fired to cone 10, by Ginger Steele, dia: 20 in.

Oval Dogwood Platter, earthenware, painted slips, sgraffitto, slip trailing, fired to cone 03, by Benjamin Carter, length: 20½ in.

Platter Inspired by Bollywood, formed over drape mold, textured, decorated with a combination of underglazes and slip, fired to cone 6, by Charan Sachar.

Gallery

Black & Gold Plate, black and bronze glazes, fired to cone 10, oxidation, by Barbara Brown.

There It Begins, earthenware decorated with tape, paper resist, terra sig, smoke-fired, by Russel Fouts.

Nesting Platters, textured slabs slumped in a hollow wooden form, coil rims, handles, and feet added, glaze wiped back to remain in texture, fired to cone 6, electric, by Lauren Bellero, length: 18 in.

From a Slab of Clay

Tray, stamped assembled slabs, slips, wood-fired, by Margaret Seidenberg-Ellis.

Large jar, decorated with a combination of underglazes and slip, fired to cone 6, by Charan Sachar.

Serving trays, textured with embossed paper, slumped in wooden bowl, fired to cone 10 in light reduction, by Ellen Currans, length: to 15 in.

George's Shrine, earthenware, ceramic decals, wax, by Patrick Coughlin, ht: 17 in.

From a Slab of Clay

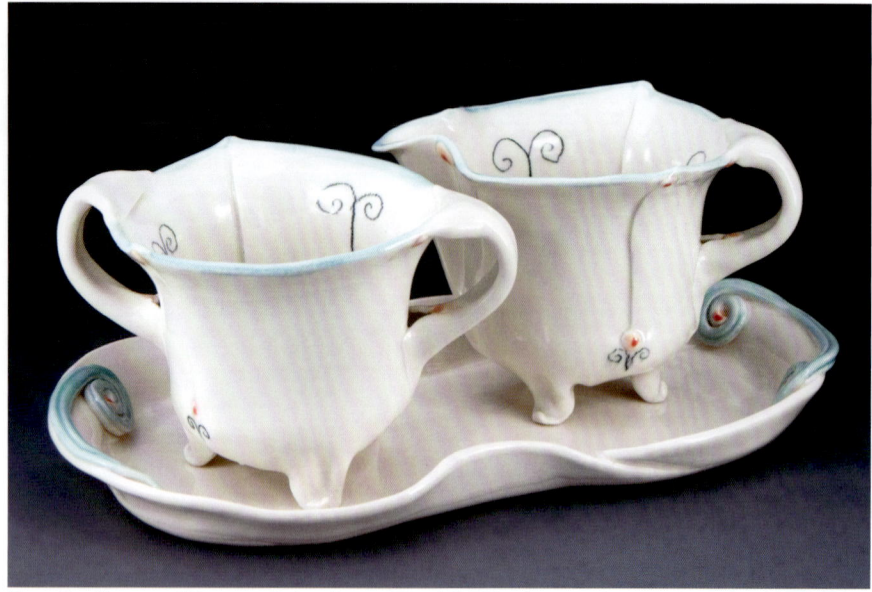

Tippy Toe Sugar and Creamer Set, soft porcelain slabs joined over a drape mold, underglazes and underglaze pencil, fired to cone 9, oxidation, by Carol Barclay.

Tea in the Tower, stoneware fired to cone 10, by David Bellar, ht: 12 in.

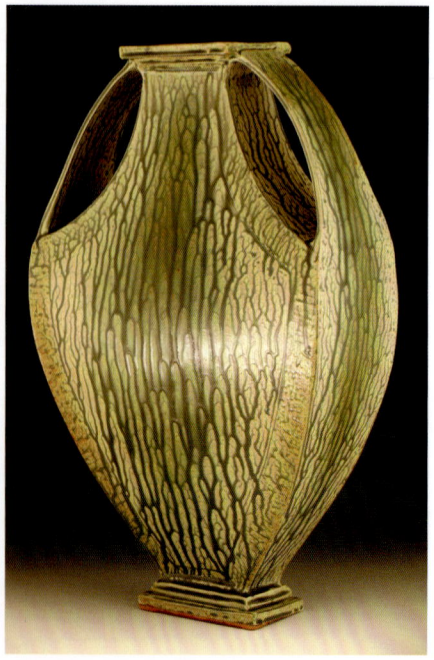

Slab-built urn, white stoneware with green ash glaze, by David Bellar, ht: 23 in.

Gallery

Serving dish, slab-built, stamped interior, extruded rim and handles, fired to cone 7-8, oxidation, by Patricia Watkins, width: 11 in.

Green Cup Set with Stand, soda fired to cone 6, by Vince Pitelka, photo by John Lucas, Tennessee Tech Photo Services

From a Slab of Clay

Barn Butter Dish, hard slab construction with press molded additions, by Patrick Coughlin, ht: 7 in.

Treasure Box, textured slabs, slip decoration, salt-fired to Cone 10., by Ginger Steele, length: 11 in.

Gallery

Conversation In Gear, stoneware, mixed media, fired to cone 6, by Sandra Benscoter, photo by Craig Phillips,

Elements In Triplicate, altered and textured stoneware slab construction, raku fired, natural material additions, by Sandra Benscoter, photo by Craig Phillips.

Black Cache Box, deeply carved then brushed with terra sigilatta at bone dry stage, bisque fired to cone 06 and black fired to cone 012, by Rose Bauer, ht: 5 in.

From a Slab of Clay

Fluidity, stoneware box, altered, glazed, gas fired, then electric fired, by Sandra Benscoter, photo by Craig Phillips.

Box, assembled textured slabs, multiple-colored slips applied then sanded off, by Margaret Seidenberg-Ellis,

Gallery

Scroll Vase, white stoneware fired to cone 10 in a gas kiln, by Larry Kruzan, ht: 18 in.

Pedestal bowl, by Kelly McLendon, originally made for use as fruit bowls, but now used as orchid pots and ikebana arrangements. Also used as serving dishes and candle holders. Fired to cone 10,

External Heart: Cody's Urn, slab built with thrown knob, added feet, cut in lid, terra sigillata surface with red terra sig pattern, soft burnished, pit fired, by Lauren Bellero, length: 11 in.

Gallery

Pit-fired Pillow, slab built with thrown parts, terra sig surface with red terra sig pattern, soft burnished, by Lauren Bellero, width: 8 in.

Dart Vase, textured slab construction, fired to cone 5 oxidation, by Alice DeLisle.

Human Wormhole 1, underglaze pencils, low fire glazes, raku fired\, by Molly Brauhn.

Oval tray, majolica on terra cotta, oxidation fired cone 03, by Linda Arbuckle, length: 12 in.

129

Square Teapot with Bamboo Handle, fired to cone 6, by Doreen Lleras, ht: 8½ in.

Mountain Tea, tarpaper used to support the slabs during construction, glazed and soda fired to cone 10, by Ruth Sachs.

Gallery

Teapot, textured with hand-made rollers, slip decoration, salt-fired to cone 10, by Ginger Steele, ht" 12 in. Built using conic templates, spout formed on a mandrel. were used to build this teapot. Clay for the spout was textured then formed on a mandrel.

From a Slab of Clay

Rex T-Set Trio, hand stamped and rolled textures, stained and glazed, by Susan Speck.

Oil Can Teapot with iron ring, bail handle, and wood grip; soda fired to cone 6, by Vince Pitelka, photo by John Lucas, Tennessee Tech Photo Services.

Gallery

Goddess Mask, wall hanging, slab-formed over face mask, terra sigillata surface with red terra sig pattern, soft burnished, pit fired, by Lauren Bellero, width: 14 in.

Icosahedron, stoneware with hand carved elemental, precision, geometric imagery, iron oxide accents, fired to cone 10 reduction, by Kyle Osvog, photo by Wayne Torborg.

First Snow, wood fired, referencing the Hoo-doos of Southern Utah and Alberta, by Tony Clennell.

Iron 2×2, terra cotta, low-fire oxidation, by Lynn Duryea, ht: 15 in. Photo by Troy Tuttle.

Tea House II, red earthenware, iron oxide stain and low-fire glazes, fired to cone 05, by Joe Szutz.

Shrine, earthenware, ceramic decals, wax, by Patrick Coughlin, ht: 15 in.

Gallery

In the Mire She Was There, mid-range earthenware, mixed media and glazed surface, cone 6 electric firing, by Liz Bryant, ht: 13 in.

From a Slab of Clay

Yellow Pillow, molded soft slabs assembled leather-hard, slip decoration after assembly, fired to cone 6, oxidation, by Joanna Stecker.

Concave Hyperbolic Jar, stoneware, soda-fired to cone 10, by Fred Sweet, ht: 15 in. Photo by Jim Stover & Fred Sweet.

Cuneatus, stiff slab construction, burnished, resist slip, glaze, raku fired, by Allyson May.

Gallery

Colander with plate, earthenware, painted slips, sgraffitto, slip trailing, fired to cone 03, Benjamin Carter, dia: 10 in.

Wood-fired Box, stoneware, wood-fired to cone 11, by Fred Sweet, ht: 10 in.

Kangaroo & Joey, made from one slab (see Demo 14), by Bill Klein.

Vegetarian, hump-molded earthenware, underglazes, fired to cone 05, by Judith Berk King.

Basket Vase, stoneware with crawl glaze, cone 10 reduction, by Doris Fischer-Colbrie, dia: 11 in., photo by John Brennan

Small box, slabs decorated with slip then assembled. When firm, the lid was cut from the box and a gallery and feet were added. Fired to cone 6, oxidation, by Margaret Seidenberg-Ellis,

Gallery

Ewer, decorated with incising and hand-made rollers, slips, by Ginger Steele, ht: 17 in.

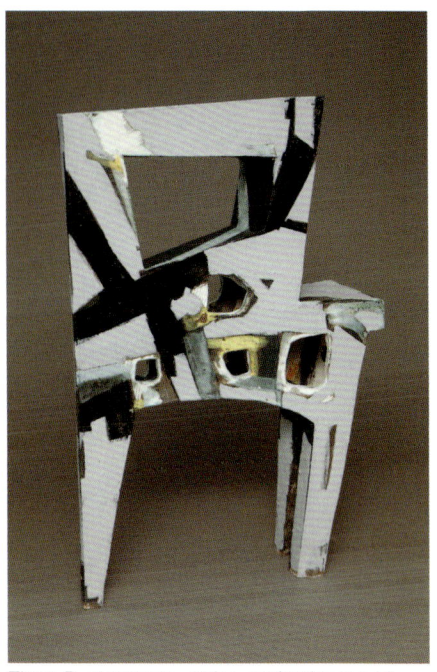

Three D, stoneware, stains, underglazes and glazes, multiple firings, acrylics, by Joe Szutz,

Toward Light, porcelain paper clay, fern textures, extruded trim, copper oxide and white glaze details, by Jiri Lonsky, photo by Allen Cheuvront

Trenes II (Trains II), low-fire clay, fired to cone 05 electric, by Elizabeth Dychter, ht: 16½ in. Photo by Martin Helman

Bowl, earthenware coated with terra sigillata then smoke-fired in an electric kiln, by Russel Fouts, dia: 15 in.

Handbuilt creamer and sugar jar, textured slabs, slip decoration, salt-fired to Cone 10, by Ginger Steele, ht: 5 in.

Gallery

Large Leaf Bowl, inspired by hosta leaves, individual clay slabs layered in a wok, carved and slip trailed, sprayed glazes, fired to cone 6 electric, by Lauren Bellero, width: 18 in.

Calla Bowl, assembled from five soft porcelain slabs, joined wet in a slump mold. Callas also formed from slabs. Fired to cone 9 oxidation, by Carol Barclay, dia: 11 in.

Underbelly of a Print, clay monotype, underglazes, stains and glaze, fired to cone 6, by Sandra Benscoter, photo by Craig Phillips.

The Devil & The Chicken, Slab-built, hump molded earthenware platter with underglazes, fired to cone 04, by Bryan Hiveley.

Long Life Vase, matte black glaze, fired to cone 10 oxidation, by Barbara Brown.

Gallery

Box, low-fire clay, fired to cone 05 then glazed and fired to cone 04, all parts cut from a slab of clay, by Simone Kestelman, ht: 4 in.

Elevator door surround, hand sculpted tiles, glazed and fired to cone 6, oxidation, by Nan Kitchens, ht: approx. 10 ft. Photo by Tom Corcoran